Edgar L. Spencer

The Great Rock Island Cook Book

Comprising a carefully compiled selection of the most useful recipes and other valuable information in the culinary art

Edgar L. Spencer

The Great Rock Island Cook Book
Comprising a carefully compiled selection of the most useful recipes and other valuable information in the culinary art

ISBN/EAN: 9783744795586

Printed in Europe, USA, Canada, Australia, Japan

Cover: Foto ©Lupo / pixelio.de

More available books at **www.hansebooks.com**

The Great Rock Island

COOK BOOK

COMPRISING A

CAREFULLY COMPILED SELECTION OF THE MOST USEFUL RECIPES
AND OTHER VALUABLE INFORMATION IN THE
CULINARY ART.

Many famous Cooks and Caterers, having contributed their favorite formulæ, which are now given to the public for the first time.

WITH THE GREATEST RESPECT THIS BOOK IS

Dedicated to the Women of America,

BY THE GENERAL TICKET AND PASSENGER DEPARTMENT OF THE CHICAGO, ROCK ISLAND & PACIFIC RAILWAY.

Entered according to Act of Congress in the year 1884,
By B. F. BABCOCK,
In the office of the Librarian of Congress, at Washington.

CHICAGO:
THE J. M. W. JONES STATIONERY AND PRINTING COMPANY.
1884.

NO POISON IN THE PAST

—IF—

DR. PRICE'S
SPECIAL FLAVORING EXTRACTS

ARE USED.

Vanilla, Lemon, Orange, Flavor Cakes, Creams, Puddings, as delicious and natural as the fruit from which they are made.

For Strength, Purity and True Fruit Flavor They Stand Alone.

FOR SALE BY ALL GROCERS.

✦Light Healthy Bread✦

—USE—

DR. PRICE'S
Lupulin Yeast Gems

THE BEST DRY HOP YEAST IN THE WORLD.

Bread raised by this yeast it light, white and wholesome, like our Grandmother's delicious bread.

Ask your Grocer for Dr. Price's Lupulin Yeast Gems.

Lupulin is the active principle of hops.

NOTICE.—Dr. Price's Cook Book, full of good things for everybody, sent by mail, free of charge, by addressing

DR. V. C. PRICE, Chicago.

The Hartford Sewing Machine

The most lavishly decorated; the largest under arm; positive or spring take-up as desired; free from vibration.

OUR MOTTO FOR FIFTEEN YEARS,

SIMPLE, CAPABLE, DURABLE.

AGENTS WANTED, TERRITORY PROTECTED.

Send for Descriptive Circulars, Terms, etc.

Ball Bearing Balance Wheel, Knife-Edge Treadle Bearing, Self-Setting Needle, Patent Belt Replacer, A Galaxy of New Patents, Artistic Designs of Wood Work.

GENERAL WESTERN OFFICE,

WEED SEWING MACHINE CO.

179 MICHIGAN AVENUE (LELAND HOTEL),

WM. M. DURELL, Manager,

CHICAGO, ILL.

Office of the New Gas Company,

94 DEARBORN STREET.

THE CONSUMERS

Gas Fuel & Light Co.

OF CHICAGO, ILLINOIS,

Solicit the patronage of the Public, and hope by fair dealing and courteous treatment to obtain it.

They are offering their beautiful Gas, which is free from sulphur compounds and other impurities, and which will not smoke the ceilings, at

$1.25 Per 1,000 Cubic Feet, net.

They make no charge for services or setting meters.

They require no deposits.

They will make contracts for five years at the above price per 1,000.

They believe in giving a good Gas at a low price.

The public, in sustaining them, are protecting their own interests.

INTRODUCTION.

"In compelling man to eat, that he may live,
Nature gives appetite to invite and pleasure to reward him."—BRILLIAT-SAVARIN.

EPICURUS, the Greek philosopher, taught that "the great end and aim of life was to eat," which doctrine was so far accepted by the luxurious Romans at a later period, as to call forth the denunciations of Cicero in the Senate, warning them that it would lead to the effeminacy of the nation. Whether or not the fall of the great Roman Empire can be attributed to the appetites of its citizens, it is unquestioned that they certainly *loved to eat*, as instance the fabulous sums expended at their banquets, where peacocks' tongues, humming-birds on toast, and other equally expensive dainties were consumed and fortunes lavished. The pleasures of the table since that time have been the first indulgence of all civilized nations.

To prepare food in the best and most wholesome manner with economy, celerity and taste, is a science in which the French especially excel; being the result of the collective ingenuity and skill of persons, who, as chéfs, have given it the study of their lives. It may be said that they literally *waste nothing*, as some method is provided for utilizing much that in an American kitchen, either through ignorance or carelessness, is destroyed.

The words of the late Prof. Blot, founder of the New York Cooking Academy, in his advice to cooks, were: "Be careful, clean and punctual. Make use of everything good. Waste nothing, however little it may be. Have no prejudices."

In presenting this little work to the housewives of America, its projectors are not possessed with the idea that the subject of cookery has not already received great attention; indeed, as the old adage teaches, "too many cooks spoil the broth," it may be said that there are already *too* many; but it is thought that this humble tribute to culinary literature will, by its arrangement and careful compilation, add something of value to the subject.

In selecting the recipes, under the different headings and sub-divisions, the aim has been to give only those which have been practically tested, derived from the best authorities, or from cooks skilled in the profession. Many have also been obtained through the courtesy of friends who have contributed favorite recipes, and are now for the first time published. Credit has been given, however, only when derived from public sources.

The object being to adapt it more to the household, it has not been considered as within its province to cater to the epicure, hence the more elaborate, highly seasoned, or costly dishes, with few exceptions, have been omitted.

As our efforts have been directed to serve the new as well as the more mature housekeeper, and with the view to economy in the purchase of the multifarious articles comprising "household supplies," there are presented *notes*, more or less extended, preceding the recipes of each division, giving, concisely as possible, information relating to the selection or keeping of provisions, regarding adulterations, or general directions as to modes. In many cases, also, the basis for forming a great number of dishes or productions have been given, instead of numerous distinct recipes, leaving it to the taste or ingenuity of the intelligent housewife to produce those—by the variation of ingredients or process—best suited to the season, the purse or occasion. With the same view, also, several recipes have in many cases been given for the same dish.

Believing the work would prove of more value thereby, greater attention has been bestowed on substantials. Much less room has been allotted to cake, pastry, pickles, preserves, etc., than to meats, fish, poultry or vegetables; while to bread-making and its concomitants considerable space has been afforded.

It is thought that the plan of consecutively numbering the recipes will prove convenient, as well as the classified index at the back of the book.

Should even our efforts so far have succeeded as to aid the women of our country in preparing more acceptable dishes, or at less expenditure, and thus adding to their material wealth, our task will be but imperfectly fulfilled without at the same time reminding them as well as the traveling public that

The Great Rock Island Route

WITH ITS SUPERB EQUIPMENT OF

ELEGANT COACHES, PALATIAL SLEEPING,

LUXURIANT DINING AND EASY RECLINING-CHAIR CARS,

ITS SAFETY APPLIANCES, SMOOTH STEEL TRACKS AND RELIABLE CONNECTIONS,

Is preëminently the best, not only for *all points located upon, but beyond it.*

⇒The Great Medical Wonder,⇐
HAMLIN'S WIZARD OIL,
FOR INTERNAL AND EXTERNAL USE.

The great reputation which this remedy has attained, must be attributed solely to ITS REAL VALUE. A worthless medicine, when stimulated by advertising, will sell for a time; but, as soon as allowed to depend upon solid merit, it drops out. f the market entirely. This is not the case with HAMLIN'S WIZARD OIL. When once introduced into any section of country, it never dies out. Its sale is constantly increasing, and at the present time has assumed such proportions as to justify us in the assertion that it has never been equaled by any other remedy.

In almost every city, town, or village, from the Atlantic Ocean to the Pacific, and from the State of Maine to the Gulf of Mexico, HAMLIN'S WIZARD OIL is known and appreciated, and in thousands of families has become a household necessity. The large number of REMARKABLE CURES which have been performed through the instrumentality of this great remedy, are unparalleled in the history of medicine. Hundreds of supposed cripples for life, and sufferers who have languished upon beds of sickness, receiving no aid from physicians, testify to its wonderful healing properties.

It not only allays inflammation, and STOPS THE MOST EXCRUCIATING PAINS, but it performs radical and PERMANENT CURES. It is safe and sure, does its work quickly and effectually, and is just the article needed in every family.

IT CURES

Rheumatism in from one to six days; Neuralgic Pains in ten minutes; Headache or Earache in ten minutes; Toothache in one minute; Sore Throat in three hours; Diphtheria in twelve hours; Fever and Ague in one day; Pain in the Back or Side in thirty minutes; Contracted Cords and Muscles, and all Painful Swellings and Tumors, Sprains, Bruises, Cuts, Burns and Scalds, Ulcers, Fever Sores, Cramp-Colic, Diarrhœa and Cholera Morbus, Dyspepsia, Inflammation of the Kidneys, Catarrh in the Head, Deafness, Stiff and Enlarged Joints, and all Diseases of an Inflammatory Nature.

Unequaled for Burns and Scalds.

PREPARED AT THE LABORATORY OF
HAMLINS WIZARD OIL CO., CHICAGO, ILL.
PRICE, 50 CENTS AND $1.00 PER BOTTLE.
FOR SALE BY ALL DRUGGISTS.

FERMENTUM

THE ONLY RELIABLE

COMPRESSED YEAST

Is produced from No. 1 Grain, and Manufactured only by the

RIVERDALE DIST. COMPANY

OFFICE AND WAREHOUSE:

264 to 270 Kinzie Street,

CHICAGO, ILLS.

A. JUNKER, - - - General Agent.

To produce the lightest and best **BREAD, BISCUIT**, or **ROLLS**, use "**FERMENTUM**" and the following **RECIPES**:

WHEAT BREAD—(for 4 Loaves)—Thoroughly dissolve a Cake of FERMENTUM in a pint of lukewarm water; stir in sifted flour until it forms a thick batter as for Cakes; set in a warm place until it rises and begins to settle; then add to this sponge a quart of lukewarm water, a tablespoon salt, two of sugar, the same of butter, with sifted flour to make a dough as soft as can be handled, and knead it well. Set it to rise and when thoroughly light knead it thoroughly again, form into loaves and place in greased pans for final rising. When sufficiently light, bake in a moderately quick oven. When baked, cool the loaves by standing them on ends, leaning against each other, in a cool place.

BISCUITS OR ROLLS.—Use a half cake of FERMENTUM to each quart of flour; dissolve it thoroughly; add the flour and mould at once; set in a warm place and bake in a brisk oven as soon as light.

Ask your Grocer for **FERMENTUM**, and accept no other Yeast or Raising Compound whatever. **FOR SALE EVERYWHERE.**

BREAD.

1. Stock Yeast—Boil three ounces hops in three quarts water for half an hour. Put a handful of dry sifted flour into a stone jar, and scald it with enough of the hop water to make a stiff paste and set aside. Let the rest of the hop water boil slowly for an hour and a half, strain it on the paste without stirring, and set aside to cool. When blood-warm add a small handful of malt, mix well; tie a cotton cloth over it and let it stand untouched in a moderately cool place, for forty-eight hours; then bottle, and keep in a cool, dark cellar.

2. Stock Yeast—On Monday morning boil one pint hops in two gallons water for half an hour, strain into a crock and let it become lukewarm, add two even teaspoons salt and half a pint best brown sugar, mix half a pint flour smooth with some of the liquor, and stir all well together. On Wednesday add three pounds boiled and mashed potatoes, stir well, and let stand until Thursday, then strain and put in jugs, but for the first day or two leave the corks loose. Stir the yeast occasionally while making and keep near the fire. It should be made two weeks before using, and will be improved by age. Keep it in a cool place, and shake the jug before pouring from it—but with the cork out—holding the palm of the hand over the mouth.

3. Potato Yeast—Peel and boil four or five large potatoes, mash them fine, add a tablespoon of flour, a pinch each of sugar and salt, and when blood-warm add one and a half gills of the stock yeast, and let it ferment six hours, when it will be ready for use.

4. Potato Yeast—Take as many hops as can be grasped in the hand twice, put half a gallon water over them in a new coffee pot kept for that purpose, boil slowly for one hour. Do not tie them in a cloth to boil, as the above is a superior method. Pare and grate half a dozen large potatoes into a two-gallon stone crock, add a half cup sugar and a tablespoon each of salt and ginger, pour over this a half gallon of the boiling hop water, stirring all the time. When milk-warm add one cup good lively yeast, set in a warm place until it rises, and then remove to the cellar or some cool place. The hop water must be added to the potatoes *immediately*, or they will darken and discolor the yeast. To prevent them from darkening, the potatoes may be grated into a pan half filled with cold water, as they will sink to the bottom; when done grating, pour off the water and add the boiling hop water. This is a valuable recipe, and the manner of boiling the hop water is especially recommended.

5. Potato Yeast without Hops—Take four good-sized potatoes, peeled, boiled and mashed, four tablespoons white sugar, one of ginger, one of salt, and two cups flour; pour over this a pint of boiling water, and beat until all the lumps disappear. After it has cooled sufficiently add to it one cup good yeast, and set away to rise; when it has risen put in a glass or stone jar, cover and set it away in a cool place for use.

6. Hop Yeast—Boil a large handful of hops in two quarts water for twenty minutes; strain one half of it on three pints of sifted flour, and when the other half is cool, mix slowly with the paste; stir in half a pint of fresh, strong brewers' yeast, or use yeast of a previous making; bottle and cork loosely, and let it ferment until it ceases to work; next day cork tightly, and set in a cool cellar. Make fresh every week.

7. Yeast Cake—Boil half a pound of hops in one gallon water until reduced to two quarts; strain it, mix in wheat flour enough to make a thin batter, and add half a pint of fresh, strong yeast. When fermented, work with Indian meal to a stiff dough. Cover and set in a warm place to rise. When light, roll into a sheet an inch thick, and cut into small cakes, three inches across, spread them on a platter, and dry in a cool shade. Turn them several times a day, and when dry, put them in paper bags, and set in a closely covered box, and keep cool in a perfectly dry place. Use one cake for four quarts flour.

8. To Cool Bread—Bread should be always carefully cooled before being put away, especially if kept in a tight box or crock, and for this purpose a board should be kept—oaken being the best, as being solid and odorless—cover with a white flannel cloth, and over this spread a fresh linen bread cloth. Place the bread upon this, crust-side up, and cover with some thin material to keep off the flies. Place in a cool airy place. Bread cooled in this manner will have a fine soft crust, and remain light and wholesome.

9. Hop Yeast Bread—One tea cup yeast, three pints warm water; make a thin sponge at tea time, cover and let it remain two hours, or until very light. By adding water to the flour first, and having the sponge quite warm, it is never necessary to put it over hot water or in an oven to make it rise. Knead into a loaf before going to bed; in the morning mold into three loaves, spread a little lard between as they are put in the pan. When light, bake one hour, having the oven quite hot when the bread is put in, and very moderate when it is done. Bread made in this manner is never sour or heavy.

BISCUIT OF SAME SPONGE—To have fine, light biscuit, add to a portion of the sponge for bread shortening at night, and in the morning make into biscuit, and bake for breakfast.

10. Twice-Raised Bread—Measure out four quarts of sifted flour, take out a pint in a cup and place the balance in a bread-pan; make a hole in the heap of flour, into which turn one tablespoon of sugar, one of salt and one cup of yeast, previously mixed with the pint of flour; then mix in one pint of milk which has been made blood warm by adding one pint of boiling water; beat well with a strong spoon, add one tablespoon lard, knead for twenty or thirty minutes and let it rise over night; in the morning knead again and make into loaves; let them raise one hour and bake fifty minutes.

Water may be used instead of the pint of milk, in which case use twice as much lard.

11. Boston Brown Bread—One pint each of rye or Graham and Indian meal, one cup molasses, three-fourths cup sour milk, one and a half teaspoons soda, one and a half pints cold water; put on stove over cold water, which gradually bring to a boil; steam for four hours and place in the oven to brown over. All steam-cooked breads are the better for the above method of steaming.

12. Boston Brown Bread—Two cups white flour, two of Graham flour, one cup Indian meal, one teaspoon soda, one cup molasses, three and a half cups milk, a little salt. Beat well and steam for five hours.

13. Corn Bread (Of the St. Charles Hotel, New Orleans)—Beat two eggs very light; mix with them one pint either sour or buttermilk, and one pint *yellow* sifted Indian meal. Melt one tablespoon of butter with one teaspoon of salt and add to the mixture. Dissolve one teaspoon soda in a small portion of the milk and add the last thing. Beat all up very hard and bake in a pan in a brick oven for about three-quarters of an hour.

14. Corn Bread—One pint corn meal, one-half teaspoon soda, one teaspoon cream tartar, one-half teaspoon salt, one egg, and milk enough to form a stiff batter. Bake in a hot oven. The tins in which you bake should be hot and well greased before putting in the batter.

15. Corn Bread—One pint corn meal, sifted; one pint wheat flour, one pint sour milk, two eggs beaten lightly, half a cup sugar, a piece of butter size of an egg; add lastly one teaspoon soda in a little milk; add to the beaten egg the milk and meal alternately, then the butter and sugar. If sweet milk is used, add one teaspoon cream-tartar. Bake for twenty minutes in a hot oven.

16. Steamed Corn Bread—Two cups each of Indian meal, Graham flour and sour milk, two-thirds cup of molasses, one teaspoon soda. Mix well and steam two hours and a half.

17. Boston Corn Bread—One cup of sweet milk, two of sour milk, two-thirds cup of molasses, one of wheat flour, four of corn meal and two teaspoons soda; steam for three hours, and brown a few minutes in the oven.

18. Graham Bread—Use a little over a quart of warm water, one-half cup brown sugar or molasses, one-fourth cup hop yeast, and one and a half teaspoons salt; thicken the water with unbolted flour to a thin batter; add sugar, salt and yeast, and stir in more flour until quite stiff. In the morning add a small teaspoon soda, and flour enough to make a batter as stiff as can be stirred with a spoon; put it into pans, and let rise again; then bake in an even hot oven, not too hot at first; keep warm when rising; smooth over each loaf with a knife or spoon dipped in hot water.

19. Rye and Indian Bread—One quart rye meal or rye flour, two quarts Indian meal, scalded (by placing in a pan and pouring over it just enough *boiling* water to merely wet it, but not enough to make it into a batter, stirring constantly with a spoon), one-half cup molasses, two teaspoons salt, one of soda, one tea cup yeast; make it as stiff as can be stirred with a spoon, mixing with warm water, and let rise all night; then put it in a large pan, smooth the top with the hand dipped in cold water; let it stand a short time, and bake five or six hours. If put in the oven late in the day, let it remain all night.

Graham may be used instead of rye, and baked as above.

This is similar to the "Rye and Injun" of our grandmother's days, but that was placed in a kettle, allowed to rise, then placed in a covered iron pan upon the hearth before the fire, with coals heaped upon the lid, to bake all night.

20. Rye Bread—Make a sponge of one quart warm water, one tea-cup yeast thickened with rye flour; put in a warm place to rise over night. Scald one pint corn meal; when cool add it to the sponge. Add rye flour until thick enough to knead, but *knead it but little*; let rise, mould into loaves, place in deep pie-tins or small square pudding-pans, let it rise, and bake; or thicken the sponge with rye flour, and proceed as above.

21. Rye Bread—Make a sponge as for wheat bread, let it rise over night, then mix it up with rye flour (but not so stiff as wheat bread), and bake.

22. Salt-Raised Bread—The leaven for this bread is thus prepared: Take a pint of warm water at about 90 deg. (if only a little too hot you will not succeed), in a perfectly clean bowl, and stir up a thick batter, adding but a teaspoon of salt; beat very thoroughly—this is important. Set it in a pan of warm water to secure uniformity of temperature, and in from two to four hours it will begin to rise. The rising is much more sure if coarse flour or "shorts" is used instead of fine flour.

When your "rising" is nearly light enough, take a pint of milk and a pint of boiling water (a tablespoon of lime water added is good, and frequently prevents souring), mix the sponge in the bread-pan, and when cooled to about milk-warm, stir in the rising. The sponge thus made will be light in two to four hours with good warmth. The dough requires less kneading than yeast-raised dough.

To ascertain the temperature of the water in preparing the rising, place a thermometer in for a minute or so.

Some object to this bread on account of its odor when rising, the result of fermentation, but the more there is of this the surer you will be of having a good sweet bread when baked.

23. Bread Sponge for Winter Use—Peel and boil four or five medium-sized potatoes in two quarts of water (which will boil down to about one quart by the time the potatoes are cooked); when done, take out and press through a colander, or mash very fine in the crock in which the sponge is made; make a well in the center, into which put one cup of flour, and pour over it the boiling water from the potatoes; stir thoroughly, and when cool add a pint of tepid water, flour enough to make a thin batter, and a cup of yeast. This sponge makes very moist bread.

BREAKFAST AND TEA CAKES.

Note.—Soda, Saleratus (or pearlash), cream of tartar and baking powders are often adulterated with terra alba (white earth).
Some baking powders contain alum, and such are to be avoided as deleterious. Use only those of known merit, such as are manufactured by well known and reputable Houses.

24. Graham Gems—A pint of sour or butter-milk, one teaspoon soda and a little salt; beat all well together and add one egg, a tablespoon of molasses, and Graham flour sufficient to make a stiff batter; mix thoroughly. Bake in gem-pans well greased and quite hot, in a quick oven.

25. Graham Gems—Three cups sour milk, one teaspoon soda, one of salt, one tablespoon brown sugar, one of melted lard, one beaten egg; to the egg add the milk, then the sugar and salt, then the Graham flour (with the soda mixed in), together with the lard; make a stiff batter so it will *drop*, not pour from the spoon. Have the gem pans very hot, fill and bake fifteen minutes in a hot oven.

26. Wheaten Gems—Mix one teaspoon baking powder and a little salt into a pint of flour; add to the beaten yelks of two eggs one cup sweet milk or cream, a piece of melted butter half the size of an egg, the flour with baking powder and salt mixed, and the well beaten whites of the two eggs. Beat well, bake immediately in gem pan in a hot oven, take out quickly, and send to table immediately.

27. Sweet Milk Gems—Beat one egg well, add a pint of new milk, a little salt, and Graham flour until it will drop off the spoon nicely; heat and butter the gem pans before dropping in the dough. Bake in a hot oven twenty minutes.

28. Indian Gems—Mix quickly a quart of Indian meal with sufficient water to make a thick batter; add a teaspoon of salt and stir thoroughly. Have ready your gem pans well greased and heated. Bake in a quick oven until nicely browned on top, and send to table hot.

29. Wheat Muffins—Mix one pint milk, two eggs, three tablespoons yeast and a saltspoon of salt, with flour enough to make a stiff batter; let rise four or five hours and bake in muffin rings in a hot oven for about ten minutes.

30. Graham Muffins—Use Graham instead of wheat flour, as above, and add two tablespoons molasses.

31. Corn Muffins—One quart sifted Indian meal, a heaping teaspoon butter, one quart milk, a saltspoon of salt, a third of a cup yeast, a tablespoon of molasses; let it rise for four or five hours and bake in muffin rings.

32. Puffet—Two eggs, well beaten, two tablespoons sugar, a piece of butter the size of an egg; beat all together quite thin; add one pint sweet milk. When all are well mixed, add one quart flour and two tablespoons baking powder previously sifted together. Have your pans well greased and hot; bake quickly. Very nice for tea.

33. Pop-Overs—Four eggs, four cups flour, four cups milk, a small piece of butter, a little salt. Bake in gem-pans, and serve with sweet sauce.

34. Cinnamon Cake—When making yeast bread and the sponge is ready to knead, take a sufficient portion and roll out three-fourths of an inch thick, put thin slices of butter on the top, sprinkle with cinnamon, and then with sugar; let it rise well and bake for breakfast. Is a fine coffee cake.

35. Biscuit—Dissolve one rounded tablespoon of butter in a pint of hot milk; when lukewarm stir in one quart of flour, add one beaten egg. a little salt, and a tea-cup yeast; work the dough until smooth. If in winter set in a warm place, if in summer a cool place, to rise. In the morning work softly, and roll out a half inch thick, cut into biscuit and set to rise for thirty minutes, when they will be ready to bake. These are delicious.

36. Biscuit—Take one quart sifted flour (loosely put in), two heaping teaspoons tartaric acid and one moderately heaping teaspoon soda, one teaspoon salt, and three gills of water; shape out with a spoon and the floured hand.

37. Hard Sugar Biscuit—A pound of butter, two of flour, and one of sugar, one tablespoon cinnamon, two of caraway-seeds, three gills milk, a teaspoon soda. Rub the butter into the flour, and mix in the spices; dissolve the soda in the milk, mix with the sugar, and work the whole to a stiff dough. Knead it well, roll out half an inch thick, cut into round cakes, prick them with a fork, lay into buttered pans, and bake in a quick oven to a light brown.

38. Soft Sugar Biscuit—Three-fourths pound butter, three of flour, one of sugar, one quart bread sponge, milk as required. Cream together the butter and sugar, rub in the flour, then the sponge, and as much milk as will make a soft dough; knead it well, and set in a pan to rise; commence in the afternoon. Next morning knead lightly, make up with the hands into round cakes of the size of a silver dollar, and an inch in thickness. Place them an inch apart on buttered tins, set to rise in a warm place, and bake in a quick oven when light. When done brush them over lightly with a little cold water and let them cool slowly on the tins.

39. Soda Biscuit—Put one quart flour into sieve, with one teaspoon soda and two of cream tartar (or three of good baking powder), one of salt, and one tablespoon white sugar; mix all thoroughly with the flour, run through the sieve, and rub in one level tablespoon of lard or butter (or half and half of each), wet with a half pint sweet milk, roll out on board, about an inch thick, cut with a biscuit cutter or tumbler, and bake in a quick oven fifteen minutes. If you have no milk, use a little more butter or lard, and wet with water. Handle as little and make as soon as possible.

40. South Carolina Biscuit—One quart sweet cream or milk, one and a half cups butter or fresh lard, two tablespoons white sugar, one good teaspoon salt; add flour sufficient to make a stiff dough, knead well, and mould into neat, small biscuit with the hands, as our grandmothers used to do; add one good teaspoon cream tartar if preferred. Bake well and you have sweet biscuit that will keep for weeks in a dry place, and are very nice for traveling lunch.

41. Parker House Rolls—Two quarts flour, one pint cold boiled milk, half cup yeast, half cup sugar, one tablespoon melted butter; make a well in the heap of flour, pour in all the above, and let it rise until morning; then knead and let it rise until about three in the afternoon; then roll out, butter them about the edge, and lap over; raise for tea, and bake in a hot oven about twenty minutes.

42. Vienna Rolls—Have ready in a bowl a tablespoon of butter or lard, made soft by warming a little, and stirring with a spoon. Add to one quart of unsifted flour two heaping teaspoons of baking powder; mix and sift thoroughly together, and place in a bowl with the butter. Take sufficient sweet milk to form a dough of the usual stiffness, according to the flour, put into the milk half a teaspoon of salt, and then stir it into the flour, etc., with a spoon, forming the dough, which turn out on a board and knead sufficiently to make smooth. Roll out half an inch thick, and cut with a large round cutter; fold each one over to form a half-round, wetting a little between the folds to make them stick together; place on buttered pans, so as not to touch, wash over on top with milk to give them a gloss, and bake immediately in a hot oven twenty minutes. It will do them no harm to stand half an hour before baking if desired.

43. Coffee Rolls—Work into a quart of bread dough a rounded tablespoon of butter and half a cup white sugar; add some dried currants (well washed and dried in the oven), sift some flour and sugar over them, and work into the other ingredients; make into small rolls, dip into melted butter, place in tins, let rise a short time and bake.

44. Egg Rolls—Two cups sweet milk, two eggs, a little salt, three and a half scant cups sifted flour. Bake in hot gem pans.

45. Long Breakfast Rolls—Three and a half cups sweet milk, one cup butter and lard mixed in equal proportions, one cup potato yeast, flour enough to make a dough. Let rise over night; in the morning add one beaten egg. Knead thoroughly and let rise again. With the hands make into balls as large as a small hen's egg; then roll between the hands to make long rolls (about three inches), place close together in even rows in the pans. Let rise until light, and bake delicately.

46. Sally Lunn—One and one-half pounds of flour, two ounces of butter, one pint of new milk, one saltspoon salt, and three eggs, one tablespoon yeast. Warm the milk and butter over water until the butter is melted; beat the eggs in a two-quart tin pail, and if the milk is not hot pour it over them. Stir in half the flour, then add the yeast, stirring thoroughly with the rest of the flour. Let rise over night. Bake a little brown in a quick oven. Some add two tablespoons sugar and a teaspoon of soda, and two of cream tartar, instead of the yeast.

47. English Crumpets—One quart warm milk, one teaspoon salt, half cup yeast, and flour enough for a stiff batter. When light add half a cup melted butter, let stand twenty minutes, and bake in muffin rings or cups.

48. Cracknells—To a pint of rich milk put two ounces butter and a spoon of yeast. Make it warm, and mix in enough fine wheat flour to make a light dough; roll thin and cut in long pieces two inches broad. Prick well and bake in a slow oven.

49. Buns—One quart bread sponge, three pounds flour, three-fourths pound butter, one of sugar, milk as required. Make the sponge in the following manner: Into a pint of water stir enough flour to make a smooth batter, add three gills yeast, cover and put in a warm place to rise; when very light it is fit for use. In cold weather tepid water is required. Cream the butter and sugar, rub the flour in by handfuls, work smooth, add the sponge, and milk to make a soft dough; knead well, and set it to rise over night. The next morning knead it lightly and roll into sheets half an inch thick, cut into small round cakes, put them into shallow pans well buttered so they touch each other, and set them in a warm place to rise. When light bake in a quick oven. Take them out of the pan and wash them over with thin molasses and water, and dust with powdered sugar. Serve when fresh.

50. Buns—Break one egg into a cup and fill with sweet milk; mix with it half a cup of yeast, same of butter, one cup of sugar, and enough flour to make a soft dough; flavor with nutmeg; let rise until very light, then mould into biscuit with a few currants. Let them rise a second time in the baking-pan; bake, and when nearly done, glaze with a little molasses and milk.

51. London Hot Cross Buns—One and a half pints milk, half pint yeast, and sufficient flour to make a stiff batter; set this as a sponge over night, and next morning add half pound sugar, a quarter pound melted butter, half a nutmeg grated fine, one saltspoon salt, and flour to make up like biscuit; knead well and set to rise for five hours; roll half an inch thick, cut into round cakes and lay in a buttered pan. After about half an hour make a cross with a knife upon each and set at once in the oven; bake a light brown; while yet warm brush them over with the white of an egg beaten with powdered sugar quite stiff.

52. Rusk—Three pounds flour, half pound of butter, same of sugar, two eggs, a pint and a half milk, two tablespoons rose water, three do. strong yeast. Sift the sugar into a large pan, and rub it into the butter and sugar; beat the eggs very light and stir into the milk, adding the rose water and yeast. Make a hole in the dough, pour in the mixture, and slowly mix it to a thick batter; cover and set by the fire to rise. When light knead it well, cut into small cakes and knead each separately, lay them near to each other, but not touching, in shallow pans well dusted with flour; prick each one with a fork, and set in a warm place to rise again. When quite light bake in a moderate oven. They should be eaten the same day.

53. Rusk—Two cups raised dough, one of sugar, half cup butter, two well beaten eggs, flour enough to make a stiff dough; set to rise, and when light, mould into high biscuit, and let rise again; sift sugar and cinnamon over the top and place in oven.

54. Lebanon Rusk—One cup mashed potatoes, one of sugar, one of home-made yeast, three eggs; mix together; when raised light add half a cup butter or lard, and flour enough to make a soft dough; when light mould into small cakes, and let them rise again before baking. If wanted for tea, set about 9 A. M.

55. Johnny Cakes—Scald a quart Indian meal, with water enough to make a very thick batter; add two or three teaspoons salt; mould into small cakes with the hands well floured; fry them in nearly sufficient fat to cover them. When brown on the under side turn them, cooking them about twenty minutes. When done, split and butter them.

56. Johnny Cake—Two-thirds teaspoon soda, three tablespoons sugar, one teaspoon cream tartar, one egg, one cup sweet milk, six tablespoons Indian meal, three tablespoons flour, and a little salt. This makes a thin batter.

57. New England Johnny Cake—Take one pint of fine corn meal, and pour over it enough boiling water to wet it all through; add about a teaspoon salt; then pour in milk until the mixture will drop easily from the spoon; beat it well; fry on a griddle about three-quarters of an hour, turning them when nicely browned on one side.

58. Alabama Johnny Cake—Cook a pint of rice until tender, add a tablespoon butter; when cold add two beaten eggs and one pint cornmeal, and when mixed spread on an oaken board and bake by tipping the board before the fire-place. When done on one side turn over. The dough should be spread half an inch thick

59. Corn Dodgers—To one quart corn meal add a little salt and a small tablespoon lard; scald with boiling water and beat hard for a few minutes; drop in large spoonsful in a well greased pan. The batter should be thick enough to just flatten on the bottom, leaving them quite high on the center. Bake in a hot oven.

60. French Crackers—One and a half pounds each of flour and sugar, three quarters pound butter, the whites of five eggs; before baking wash over with egg and dip in sugar.

61. Egg Crackers—Six eggs, twelve tablespoons sweet milk, six tablespoons butter, half teaspoon soda; mould with flour half an hour and roll thin.

62. Economical Toast—Add to one-half pint of sweet milk two tablespoons sugar, a little salt, and a well-beaten egg; dip into this slices of bread (if dry, let it soak a little), and fry on a buttered griddle until a light brown on each side. Dry bread may thus be well used.

63. Excellent Toast—Cut slices of a uniform thickness of half an inch; move around over a brisk fire, to have all parts uniformly toasted; hold only so near the coals that the pieces will be heated through when both sides are properly browned. A light wire grid-iron will be found very convenient and enable you to toast several slices at once. If the smallest part of either of the slices are blackened or charred, carefully scrape it off, or it will flavor the whole. If covered with an earthen bowl it will keep moist and warm, or a clean towel or napkin will answer if it is to be immediately served. Stale bread may be used for milk-toast, but sweet, light bread, about a day old, is the best for dry-toast.

64. Corn-Meal Mush—Put four quarts fresh water in a kettle to boil, salt to suit the taste; when it begins to boil stir in one and a half quarts meal, letting it sift through the fingers slowly to prevent lumps, adding it a little faster at the last, until as thick as can be conveniently stirred with one hand; set in the oven in the kettle (or take out into a pan), bake an hour, and it will be thoroughly cooked. It takes corn meal so long to cook thoroughly that it is very difficult to boil it until done without burning. The thorough cooking and baking in oven afterwards, takes away all the raw taste of the meal, that is so generally found in mush prepared in the ordinary way, and adds much to its sweetness and delicious flavor.

A hard wooden paddle, two feet long, with a blade two inches wide and seven long, will be found a most convenient instrument to stir with.

65. Graham Mush—Sift Graham meal slowly into boiling salted water, stirring briskly until thick as can be stirred with one hand; serve with milk or cream and sugar, or butter and syrup. It will be improved by removing from the kettle to a pan, as soon as thoroughly mixed, and steaming three or four hours. It may also be eaten cold, or sliced and fried, like corn-meal mush.

66. Oat-Meal Mush—To two quarts boiling water, well salted, add one and a half cups best oat meal ; stir the meal in by degrees, and after stirring up a few times to prevent its settling down in a mass at the bottom, leave it to cool three hours *without stirring.* While stirring in, put the inner kettle directly on the stove. (All mushes and preparations of like description should be cooked in a custard kettle, or water bath, like a carpenter's glue-pot.) To cook for breakkfast it may be put on over night, allowing it to boil an hour or two in the evening, but it is better when freshly cooked. Serve with cream and sugar. To be wholesome it must be well cooked, slowly, but for a considerable time. In lieu of a custard kettle the mush may be made in a pan or small tin bucket, and then placed in a steamer and steamed two hours.

This is unsurpassed as a breakfast dish, and especially good for young children who need bone and muscle-producing food.

67. Steamed Oat Meal—To one teacup oat meal add a quart cold water, a teaspoon salt; put in a steamer over a kettle of cold water, gradually heat and steam an hour and a half after it begins to cook.

68. Cracked Wheat—Two quarts salted water to two teacups best cracked wheat; boil two or three hours in a custard kettle; or, soak over night and boil at least three-fourths of an hour; or, put boiling water in a pan or small bucket, set on the stove, stir in the cracked wheat, set in a steamer and steam four hours; or, make a strong sack of thick muslin or drilling, moisten the wheat with cold water, add a little salt, place in sack, leaving half the space for wheat to swell in; fit a round sheet of tin, perforated with holes half an inch in diameter, to the inside of ordinary kettle, so that it will rest two or three inches from the bottom; lay the sack on the tin, put in water enough to reach the tin, and boil from three to four hours, supplying water as it evaporates. Serve with butter and syrup or cream and sugar. When cold it is fine when sliced and fried; or, warm it with a little milk and salt, in a pan greased with a little butter; or, make into griddle cakes with a batter of eggs, milk and a little flour and a pinch of salt.

69. Fine Hominy or Grits—Take two cups hominy or wheaten grits to two quarts salted water, soak over night, and boil three-quarters of an hour in a custard kettle. Serve with milk and sugar; or, when cold, slice and fry.

GRIDDLE OR BATTER CAKES.

70. Waffles—Take one quart flour, two teaspoons good baking powder, one of salt, one of sugar, all sifted together; add a tablespoon of butter, two eggs, and a pint and a half of sweet milk; cook in waffle-irons well heated and greased.

71. Waffles—One pint flour, one of sweet milk, three eggs well beaten, a piece of butter the size of an egg and a half, a little salt, one heaping teaspoon cream-tartar, half teaspoon soda; melt the butter and stir in flour, milk and eggs. Sift the cream-tartar and soda through a fine sieve the last thing.

72. Waffles—Take one quart flour, a teaspoon salt, a tablespoon melted butter, and milk sufficient to make a thick batter; mix thoroughly; add two well-beaten eggs, two heaping teaspoons tartaric acid, and one moderately heaping teaspoon soda; stir well together, and bake at once in waffle-irons.

73. Quick Waffles—Two pints milk, one cup melted butter, and sifted flour to make a soft batter; add the well-beaten yelks of six eggs, then the beaten whites, and lastly (just before baking), four teaspoons baking powder; beat very hard and fast for a few minutes. Are very good with but four or five eggs, but much better with more.

74. Raised Waffles—One quart flour, one pint sweet lukewarm milk, two eggs, a tablespoon melted butter, a teaspoon salt and half a cup good yeast. Bake in waffle-irons well heated and greased.

75. Rice Waffles—Boil half a pint of rice and let it get cold, mix with it a quarter pound of butter, and a little salt; sift in it one and a half pints flour; beat five eggs separately; stir the yelks together with one quart milk, add the whites beaten to a stiff froth, beat hard, and bake at once in waffle-irons.

76. Massasoit House Waffle—Mix a batter with milk the thickness of buckwheat batter; raise the paste with compressed yeast; add three eggs and three spoonfuls of melted butter, and mix thoroughly. Should the batter become sour add a little soda.

77. Buckwheat Cakes—Use only buckwheat flour perfectly clear of *grits* and free from adulteration with rye or corn; warm one pint sweet milk and one pint water—or one may be cold and the other boiling—put half of this into a stone crock, add five teacups buckwheat flour, beat well until smooth, add the rest of the milk and water, and lastly a cup of yeast. Or, the same ingredients and proportions may be used, except adding two tablespoons molasses or sugar, and using one quart water instead of one pint each of milk and water.

78. Buckwheat Cakes without Yeast—Two cups of buckwheat flour, one of wheat flour, a little salt, three teaspoons baking powder; mix thoroughly, and add about equal parts of milk and water until the batter is of the right consistency, then stir until free from lumps. If they do not brown well add a little molasses.

79. Bread Griddle Cakes—One quart milk, boiling hot; two cups fine bread crumbs, three eggs, a teaspoon nutmeg, one tablespoon melted butter, one-half teaspoon salt, one teaspoon soda, dissolved in hot water; break the bread into the boiling milk and let stand for ten minutes in a covered bowl, then beat to a smooth paste; add the yelks of the eggs well whipped, the butter, salt, soda, and finally the whites of the eggs previously whipped stiff.

80. Huckleberry Griddle Cakes—Two cups milk, a cup and a half molasses, three eggs, one and a half teaspoon soda, a little salt, and flour to make a batter. Add the berries after the batter is well mixed, and bake like other griddle cakes.

81. Corn Cakes—One pint corn meal, one of sour milk or butter-milk, one egg, one teaspoon soda and one of salt. A tablespoon of corn starch may be used instead of the egg; bake on a griddle.

82. Batter Cakes—Make a batter of one quart each of flour and sour milk, three eggs beaten separately, a tablespoon of butter and a level teaspoon of soda; pulverize the soda very fine before measuring, and thoroughly mix with the dry flour; add the whites of eggs just before baking on the griddle. May be made without eggs.

83. Flannel Cakes—Heat a pint of sweet milk, and into it put two heaping tablespoons butter, let melt, then add a pint of cold milk and the well-beaten yelks of four eggs—placing the whites in a cool place; also, a teaspoon salt, four tablespoons potato yeast, and sufficient flour to make a stiff batter; set in a warm place to rise, let it stand three hours, or over night; before baking add the beaten whites; bake like any other griddle cakes. Be sure to make the batter stiff enough, for flour must not be added after it has risen, unless it is allowed to rise again.

84. Graham Griddle Cakes—One quart Graham flour, one teaspoon baking powder, three eggs, and milk or water enough to make a thin batter.

85. Rice Griddle Cakes—Boil half a cup rice; when cold, mix one quart sweet milk, the yelks of four eggs, and flour sufficient to make a stiff batter; beat the whites to a froth, stir in one teaspoon soda and two of cream of tartar, add a little salt, and lastly the whites of the eggs; bake on a griddle. Serve by spreading them while hot with butter, and also any kind of jelly or preserves; roll them up neatly cut off the ends, sprinkle with sugar, and serve quickly.

86. Pancakes—Put in an earthen pan four whole eggs, a pinch of salt, one of sugar, three spoons of flour; beat with one quart of milk. The preparation must be very light. Bake the pancakes in a frying pan, very thickly spread with butter, turn them upside down on the table, put some currant or other jelly on one side; roll them; put them on a plate; powder them with sugar, and candy with a poker, heated red hot.—*Emile Combe, Chef de Cuisine, Hotel Wellington.*

87. Indian Pancakes—One pint Indian meal, one teaspoon salt, a small teaspoon soda; pour on boiling water until thinner than mush; let it stand until cool and add the yelks of four eggs, half a cup of flour, in which has been mixed two teaspoons cream tartar; stir in as much sweet milk or water as will make the batter suitable to bake; beat the whites well and add just before baking.

88. French Pancakes—Beat together, until smooth, six eggs and a half pound flour, melt four ounces butter, and add to the batter, with one ounce sugar and half pint milk; beat until smooth; put a tablespoonful at a time into a frying-pan, slightly greased, spreading the batter evenly over the surface by tipping the pan about; fry to a light brown; spread with jelly, roll up, dust with powdered sugar and serve hot.

89. Doughnuts—Two cups sour milk, one teaspoon soda, two cups sugar, one tablespoon melted butter, three eggs and a little salt (cinnamon if desired), flour sufficient to roll; fry in hot lard sufficient to float, skim out and drain until dry.

90. Thomaston Fritters—Three eggs, one and a half cups milk, three teaspoons baking powder, and flour enough to make thicker than batter cakes; drop into hot lard and fry like doughnuts.

A Sauce for the Above—One cup sugar, two tablespoons butter, one teaspoon flour beaten together, half a cup boiling water; flavor with extract lemon and boil until clear.

91. Queen Fritters—One pint water, four ounces butter, eight ounces flour, ten eggs; boil the water and butter together in a saucepan large enough to beat the mixture in; put in the flour all at once, and stir over the fire till well cooked; let stand till warm, and add the eggs, one at a time; beat well with a spoon against the side of the pan; fry slowly in hot lard, and dust with powdered sugar.—*Palmer House, Chicago.*

92. Apple Fritters—Three eggs beaten very light, one quart milk; make a thin batter; add a little salt and the grated rind of one lemon; pare, core and slice thin one quart select tart apples; add to the batter, and cook by dropping in by spoonfuls in boiling lard; skim out with a skimmer and drain. Serve with sauce.

93. Apple Fritters—Make a batter in the proportion of one cup sweet milk to two cups flour, a heaping teaspoon baking powder, two eggs beaten separately, one tablespoon sugar and a saltspoon of salt; heat the milk a little more than milk-warm; add it slowly to the beaten yelks and sugar, then add flour and whites of the eggs; stir all together and throw in thin slices of good sour apples, dipping the batter up over them; drop into boiling hot lard in large spoonfuls with pieces of apple in each, and fry to a light brown. Serve with maple syrup, or a nice syrup made with clarified sugar.

94. Cream Fritters—One and a half pints flour, one pint milk, six well beaten eggs, half a grated nutmeg, two teaspoons salt and one pint cream. Stir the whole together enough to mix the cream; fry in small cakes.

95. Brown Bread—One pint yellow corn meal, one pint rye meal, one-half cup flour, all sifted together; add a little salt and one cup molasses; dissolve a teaspoon of soda in half a cup of hot water, and at once fill it with *cold* water; pour it on the mixed flour, etc., adding enough tepid water to make all thin; boil a cup of raisins and stir into the bread mixture; mix all well, and it is ready for the baking tins. Use a regular brown bread tin with a cover to bake it in; bake seven hours in a *moderate* oven. The bread tin should be deep, round, small at the bottom and large at the top, with a tight cover and in the form of a small ice cream mould of conical shape. Any tinner can make it at small cost.—*Palmer House, Chicago.*

FOREMOST AMONG
BAKING POWDERS

STANDS

Phosphatic Baking Powder

The Strongest and Healthiest Baking Powder made.

It is put up in Bottles, with wide mouths to admit a Spoon, and it is endorsed by EMINENT PHYSICIANS and CHEMISTS as the MOST HEALTHFUL and NUTRITIOUS BAKING POWDER KNOWN. NO SHORTENING is required when using HORSFORD'S BAKING POWDER, and it makes LIGHTER BISCUIT, BREAD, GEMS, CAKES, etc., than it is possible to produce with any other Powder. For Sale by all Dealers.

RUMFORD CHEMICAL WORKS,
Providence, Rhode Island.

BEWARE OF IMITATIONS.

KING OF SUMMER COOK STOVES

IMPROVED "NEW SUCCESS"

CIRCULAR WICK OIL STOVE, the best, the most powerful, cheapest and safest Oil Stove in the world.

BAUER BROS. & CO.,
MANUFACTURERS,
70 Dearborn Street,   CHICAGO.

BEEF.

Note—Much depends upon a good selection of beef. The fat in that grass-fed is whiter than corn-fed, that of the cow whiter than ox beef. Select that which is a clear *cherry red* after a cut has been taken off and exposed to the air a few moments. Ox beef is far preferable to cow beef, as being the sweeter and more juicy, and is also the most economical. Meat from old or poorly-fed animals has a coarse, skinny fat and a dark red lean. To test beef, press into it with the finger. If the dent rises up quickly, it is fresh and prime; but if it disappears slowly, or remains, it is inferior. For roasts the sirloin and rib pieces are mostly used. For steaks the porterhouse and sirloin are the choicest. Rounds and rump steaks are usually tough; of the former select the inner half—they have the best flavor of any, and when well pounded before broiling are quite edible. A rib steak of fat beef—cut from between the ribs, or the ribs removed—is fine, tender and juicy. Fifteen minutes to the pound and fifteen minutes over, is the rule for roasts of beef, most people preferring it (as well as mutton) underdone. Less time is required to cook than for pork, veal or lamb, which must always be very well done to be palatable, and the rule for these is twenty minutes to the pound, and twenty minutes longer. For steaks: they are cut from half an inch to an inch and a half in thickness, and are broiled well or underdone, to fancy. Broiled steaks are far preferable to fried, when the means for cooking either way are equally convenient. When fried they should as a rule be well cooked. Do not salt beef before or while cooking, as it draws out the juices, and which, in broiling especially, are thereby lost.

96. Roast Beef—Take a rib-piece or loin-roast of seven to eight pounds; wipe it thoroughly all over, lay it in the roasting-pan and baste with melted butter; put it in the well-heated stove oven, and while roasting baste it frequently with its own drippings, which will make it both brown and tender. If, when it is cooking fast, or the gravy is growing too brown, turn a glass of cooking wine into the bottom of the pan, and repeat this as often as the gravy cooks away. Such a roast needs about two hours' time to be properly done, and should be brown outside, but inside a little red. Twenty minutes less time to be used when desired quite rare. Season with salt and pepper; squeeze a little lemon juice over it, and also turn the gravy upon it after skimming off all the fat.

97. Roast Beef with Yorkshire Pudding—Select a roast in size according to the number at table—a loin or rib-piece—and roast as in preceding recipe, care being used to baste without disturbing the pudding after it is put in. Make a Yorkshire pudding to eat with it as follows: For every pint of milk take three eggs, three cups flour, and a pinch of salt; stir to a smooth batter, and pour into the dripping-pan under the meat, half an hour before it is done.

98. Ragout of Beef—For six pounds of the round take half a dozen ripe tomatoes, cut up with two or three onions, in a vessel with a tight cover; add half a dozen cloves, a stick of cinnamon, and a little whole black pepper; cut gashes in the meat, into which stuff half a pound of fat salt pork cut in square bits; place the meat upon the other ingredients, and pour over them half a cup of vinegar and a cup of water; cover tightly, and bake in a moderate oven slowly for four or five hours, and when about done, salt to taste. When done take out the meat, strain the gravy through a colander, and thicken with flour.

99. Beef a la Mode—Into a piece of the rump cut deep openings with a sharp knife; put in pieces of pork cut into dice and previously rolled in pepper, salt, cloves and nutmeg. In an iron stew-pan lay pieces of pork, sliced lemon, sliced onions, one or two carrots, and a bay-leaf; lay the meat on and put over it a piece of bread-crust as large as the hand; pour over all a half-pint wine and a little vinegar, and afterward an equal quantity of water or rich broth, until the meat is half covered; cover the dish tightly and cook until tender; take out, rub the gravy through a sieve, skim off all fat, add some sour cream, and then return to the stew-pan to cook ten minutes. If desired, the meat may be prepared some days before in a spiced vinegar or wine pickle.

100. Beefsteak, Broiled—Lay a thick tender steak upon a gridiron, well greased with butter or suet, over hot coals. When done on one side have ready a warmed platter with a little butter on it; lay the steak, without pressing it, cooked side down, so that the juices which have gathered may run on the platter, then quickly place it upon the gridiron again and cook the other side. When done place upon the platter again, spread lightly with butter, season with salt and pepper, and keep warm for a few moments over steam, but not long enough for the butter to become oily. Serve on hot plates. Garnish with sprigs of parsley, fried potato or browned potato balls, placed around the platter.

101. Beefsteak, Fried—Never fry them when you have the means to broil them at hand. When you have not, the next best method is to heat a thin frying-pan quite hot, put in a steak previously hacked or pounded with an iron maul, let it remain a few moments, loosen it with a knife, and turn quickly several times; repeat this, and when done put on a hot platter; salt, pepper, and put over it bits of butter. When more than one, pile one on top of another, and cover with a hot platter.

102. Beefsteak and Onions—Slice the onions thin and drop into cold water. Put a steak in the pan with a little suet. Skim out the onions and add to the steak, season with pepper and salt, cover tightly and put over the fire. When the juice of the onions has dried up and the steak has browned on one side, remove the onions, turn the steak, replace the onions, and fry till done.

103. Boiled Corned Beef—Soak over night if very salt, but if the beef is young and not too long corned this is not necessary. Pour over it cold water enough to cover it well after washing off the salt. The rule for boiling meats is generally twenty-five minutes to a pound, but corned beef should be placed on a part of the stove or range where it will simmer, not boil, for from four to six hours, according to size of the piece. If tough let it remain in the liquor until next day, and bring it to the boiling point just before serving. For briskets, or plate pieces, simmer until the bones are easily removed, fold over into a square or oblong piece, place a weight upon it to press, and set where it will become cold, which will give a firm solid piece to cut in slices. Save the liquor, boil it down, remove the fat, and season with pepper and sweet herbs. Pour over finely minced scraps or pieces of the beef, press the meat firmly into a mould, and place a close cover and weight upon it. When turned from the mould garnish with sprigs of parsley or celery, and serve with French mustard or pickles.

104. Corned Beef—Have especially corned by your butcher a piece of the round, after two to four steaks are taken off (according to size of the round) of about six inches in thickness; corn three to four days, with rock salt, a little saltpetre and sugar in the pickle; wrap round it as tightly as possible several coils of strong cord; boil slowly for six to seven hours in a vessel large enough to suspend it.

If desired hot, then cut the wrapping and serve. Save the liquor in the pot, and what remains from dinner replace in it; let it stand over night, or longer, when all the liquor will be absorbed by the meat.

This process will ensure the meat both finely flavored and tender, surpassing tongue for cold lunches, tea or sandwiches. An invaluable recipe.

105. Pressed Corned Beef—After serving corned beef at dinner, while yet warm, chop up fat and lean together, not necessarily very fine only so that fat and lean may be evenly mixed; stir in enough dry mustard to flavor it; put it in an oblong tapering baking-pan, and place over it (right side up) another of same size; put into this two or three flat irons for a weight and let stand over night. The next day it will turn out in a good loaf, from which nice slices can be cut.

106. Spiced Beef Relish—A pound of rare beef chopped very fine (if you have a sausage cutter put it through that), and three Boston crackers rolled and sifted; add salt and pepper to taste, one tablespoon of table sauce and a pinch of sweet marjorum, and one egg well beaten; work all together with the hands until thoroughly mixed; form into a loaf by pressing into a bowl, and turn out on a buttered tin; rub a little butter over it, and pour on a large cup of the juice of canned tomatoes; set in the oven and bake three-quarters of an hour, basting frequently with the tomato. Serve the next day, cold.

107. Beef en Ragout—Cut one or two slices of salt pork into dice, and fry until brown; pour in a little stock or water, in which cook three or four potatoes cut in slices, a sprig of parsley, thyme, and a small bay-leaf, pepper and salt. Half an hour before serving, put in slices of cold roast beef, adding a dash of vinegar if you like.

108. Roast Beef and Tomato Sauce—Have ready on a platter nicely cut slices of cold roast beef, both rare and well done; make a tomato sauce as follows: Stew ten tomatoes, with three cloves, pepper and salt, for fifteen minutes (a sliced onion and a sprig or two of parsley may also be added if the flavor is desired); strain, put on the stove in a sauce-pan, with an egg-sized lump of butter and a tablespoon of flour previously rubbed together; stir all until smooth, and pour it hot over the beef. Let stand a few minutes before serving. Canned tomatoes may be used for the sauce.

109. Fricassee of Cold Roast Beef—Cut the beef into very thin slices, shred a handful of parsley very fine, cut a small onion into quarters, and put all together in a stewpan, with a small piece of butter and some strong soup stock ; season with salt and pepper, and simmer very gently fifteen minutes, then mix in the yelks of two eggs and a teaspoon Worcestershire sauce. Rub a hot dish with a clove of garlic, and turn the fricassee into it.

110. Stewed Beef—Take a slice of rump, pound till tender, lay in an iron kettle in which have been placed slices of pork and onions with a few pepper-corns; dredge with salt, and baste with melted butter; closely cover the kettle and place over a brisk fire, and when fried to a nice brown, add a pint of cooking wine and the same of good soup stock; stew until soft; take out the meat, skim off the fat, and add a tablespoon flour smoothly mixed with broth; add more broth gradually, strain and turn over the dish of meat. If the meat is previously placed in a spiced pickle for two or three days, it will much improve it.

111. Beef Pie—Line the sides of a pudding-dish with a puff paste, as directed (see PUDDINGS AND PASTRY), lay in small slices of cold roast beef, pepper, salt, and then a few slices cold boiled potatoes. Proceed in same way until the dish is full; pour over it a cup of gravy, and the same quantity of stewed or canned tomato, cover over with the puff paste, putting a rim of it around edge of the dish, before putting on the cover. Bake half an hour.

112. Beef and Potato Pie—Cut cold roast beef or rare-done beefsteak into thin slices, and put a layer into a pie-dish; dredge in a little flour, salt and pepper, then peel and slice in one tomato with one tablespoon grated onion; put in another layer of beef and pour in enough gravy or soup stock to moisten it; have ready a large cupful of mashed potatoes, wet with enough milk to make it soft; spread this over the top of the pie and bake about twenty-five minutes. Just before taking up, rub a little butter over the top.

113. Beef Croquettes—One cup of lean beef, one of the fat, half a cup of cold boiled or fried ham, a piece of onion as large as a silver dollar, one teaspoon of salt, half a one of pepper, a pinch of sage, and a little grated lemon-peel; chop all as fine as possible, or put through a mincing machine; then heat with half a cup of stock or cold soup; add one egg well beaten. Mould into croquettes with the hand, roll in flour or fine bread crumbs, and fry in hot lard.

114. Corned Beef Hash—Chop cold corned beef, and to one cup of meat add two of cold boiled potatoes, chopped; mix in one tablespoon dry mustard and a little pepper; put an egg-sized piece of butter in a frying-pan and let it melt slowly, turning the pan so that it will be thoroughly buttered; put in the hash, pressing it down smoothly all over the pan; moisten slightly with hot water and let cook, without stirring at all, until it begins to brown on the sides, which you can tell by pressing it back from the sides, when it will be done. Turn out on a hot platter bottom side up in a cake.

115. Beef Tongue Hash—Chop the heel of a cold boiled tongue and add twice as much cold boiled potato, with enough mustard to season it; put a piece of butter as large as an English walnut into a frying-pan; shake it as it melts, so that every part may be coated; put in the hash and press it down firmly, adding enough hot water to moisten. When it begins to cook press it away from the sides of the pan, so as to have it oval form, and as soon as browned turn out on a hot platter. Garnish with pickled beet.

116. Boiled Beef Tongue—Wash a fresh tongue and just cover it with water in the pot; put in a pint of salt and a small red pepper; add more water as it evaporates, so as to keep the tongue nearly covered until done—when it can be easily pierced with a fork; take it out, and if wanted soon, take off the skin and set it away to cool. If wanted for future use, do not peel it until it is required. A pint of salt will do for three tongues, if you have that number to boil; but do not fail to keep water enough in the pot to keep them covered while boiling. If salt tongues are used, soak them over night, of course omitting the salt when boiling. Or, after peeling a tongue, place it in a saucepan with one cup of water, half a cup vinegar, four tablespoons sugar, and cook until the liquor is evaporated.

117. Spiced Beef Tongue—Rub into each tongue a mixture made of half pound sugar, a piece of saltpeter size of a pea, and a tablespoon ground cloves; put it in a brine made of three-fourths pound of salt to two quarts of water, and keep covered. Pickle two weeks, then wash well, and dry with a cloth; roll out a thin paste made of flour and water, smear it all over the tongue, and place in a pan to bake slowly; baste well with lard and hot water; when done, scrape off the paste and skin.

118. Broiled Calves' Liver—Take a fine fresh liver of a calf two to three months' old; wash and slice about one-fourth inch thick; grease a wire gridiron and broil crisp or well done, according to taste, frequently turning, but never rare or under done. Take up and well butter both sides on a hot platter, and serve hot. Has somewhat the flavor of the breast of a broiled prairie chicken.

119. Fried Liver, Breaded—Cut in thin slices and place on a platter; pour over it boiling water, which immediately turn off (this removes any strong taste from beef's liver); have ready in the pan some hot lard or beef drippings, or both; dredge the liver with rolled crackers or dry bread crumbs rolled fine and seasoned with salt and pepper; place in the pan, cover, and fry slowly until both sides are dark brown. Should be an hour in cooking, as it is better cooked slowly.

120. Fried Tripe—Take good fat honey-comb tripe, partly dry it with a cloth, dredge with flour or dip in egg and roll in fine cracker crumbs; fry in hot butter or other fat until a delicate brown on both sides; lay it on a platter, and make a gravy in the pan by adding a little vinegar to it, which pour over the tripe.

121. Fried Tripe—Make a batter by mixing gradually one cup of flour with one of sweet milk, adding a well-beaten egg and a little salt; drain the tripe, dip in the batter, and fry in hot lard or fat.

122. Fricasseed Tripe—Cut the tripe in narrow strips, put it in a little water or milk, add a good piece of butter, previously rolled in flour; season with pepper and a little salt; let it simmer slowly for some considerable time. Serve in a deep dish, and garnish with parsley chopped fine and sprinkled on top.

123. Chipolata—Slice a small onion with a tablespoon of hot butter; when fried brown, pour in a cup of cold beef or tomato soup; add one sprig of thyme, one of parsley, and a bay-leaf, with salt and pepper; when it boils, stir in a thickening of one heaping teaspoon flour, wet with cold water; add a little caramel (see CONFECTIONERY AND CAKE), and just before serving put thin slices of cold roast beef into the gravy and let them heat through. Pour on a dish, and garnish with stoned olives, parsley or celery, according to fancy.

124. Potted Beef—From what remains of a roast of beef remove all the bone and gristle; chop it fine and season with salt and a very little Cayenne pepper, also a pinch of cloves, mace and sage; boil down a little rich soup stock—with a bit of onion in it if the flavor is desired—sufficiently to form quite a hard, strong jelly when cold; while the stock is hot moisten the meat with it, and press into an earthen pot or jar; place it in a pan of hot water, and bake two hours; then put it in a cool place for use.

125. Staffordshire Beefsteak—Beat the steak a little with a rolling pin; flour and season; then fry with a sliced onion to a fine light brown; lay the steak into a stew pan, and pour as much boiling water over as will serve for sauce; stew very gently half an hour and add a spoonful of catsup before serving.

126. Stewed Chipped Beef—Heat milk and water (about half of each), and thicken with a beaten egg and a little flour; when nicely boiled, add the beef, either chipped or sliced as thin as possible, and almost immediately remove from the fire, as the less it is cooked the better; if the beef is very salt, it will need freshening in a little hot water before going into the gravy, but if not it will season it just right.

127. Courtland Beef—Mince some cold and rare roast beef including the fat; put in a small stew pan, rubbed with a clove of garlic, a little water, half a small onion, pepper and salt, and boil it until the onion is quite soft, then add the minced beef with some of its gravy, and stew gently but do not let it boil; prepare toasted bread cut in small triangular pieces and lay around the edge of a hot dish; add a little vinegar to the stew and pour over it.

128. Filet de Bœuf Chateaubriand—Take a large or double tenderloin steak and broil it; have some parisienne potatoes (see Potatoes a la Parisienne), saute with butter, which put around the dish; melt some butter in a sauce-pan, sprinkle in a little chopped parsley; add the juice of half a lemon; mix all thoroughly and pour it over the steak.— *Edward Mehl, Chef de Cuisine, Gilsey House, New York.*

129. Beef Cakes—Chop up some rare done roast beef with a little fat ham or bacon; season with pepper, salt and a little onion; mix, and make into small cakes and fry them until brown; make a gravy of soup stock, or the beef gravy which was left, thickened with browned flour.

130. Rounds of Beef—Roasted—Take a whole round of young ox beef, weighing forty to sixty pounds (according to number for which it is to be used), neatly remove the bone and trim off all gristle or superfluous fat. Wrap around it in several coils, commencing at the top and winding downward, some stout cord half as large as a pencil, draw tight and tie. Bake it in a moderate oven (a brick oven is the best) from six to eight hours, according to size, or about an hour to each ten pounds; baste it frequently with drippings and turn it over twice during the time. Test it with a long skewer or steel and when quite tender to the centre, it is done. Rub lightly over with salt and set away in a cool dry place with the wrapping left on until required for use. It should be dark brown outside and moderately rare within. Is fine for picnics or other large assemblies,

131. Hamburger Steak—Take a pound of flank or round steak, without any fat, and chop medium fine, also chop an onion quite fine and mix well with the meat; season with a little red and black pepper mixed together in proportions of one quarter of red pepper only, and fry in a little butter or lard, the latter being preferable; fry brown or a little underdone, according to taste, and as the bottom will be the most browned when served turn it out bottom side up on the platter. Garnish with celery top around the edge of the platter, and two or three slices of lemon on top of the meat. Some make it into small flat cakes or balls before frying.—*Burkey & Milan, 154 and 156 S. Clark street, Chicago.*

132. Hamburg Steak—Mince, but not too fine, some round steak, and mix with it an onion chopped fine, a little cayenne, black pepper and salt. (Some add a little currie powder, or add part of a red pepper pod, if desired hot.) When well mixed, fry in a little lard or clear drippings; when well done, dish on a small platter, and set in the oven long enough to brown over the top. Garnish with small sprigs of celery top.

L. H. TURNER,
Chicago Straw and Felt Works
STRAW BLEACHER,

70 STATE STREET, CHICAGO.

Reshaper and Finisher of all kinds of Ladies' and Gents' Silk, Felt, Straw, Panama, Leghorn and Neapolitan Hats and Bonnets. Gents' Hats, all kinds, Retrimmed. Fur Goods and Feathers Redressed.

THE "BIG FOUR."
PEERLESS PAPILLON REMEDIES
Absolutely Vegetable. Recommended by the Public. Never Failing. Perfectly Harmless.

PAPILLON SKIN CURE

Is a specific cure for Salt Rheum, Eczema, Erysipelas, Scrofula, Scaldhead, Tetter, Hives, Dandruff, Pimples, Plant-Poisoning, Ringworm, Sunburn, and all diseases of the cutaneous system, by Exudation, and not by Excretion, whereby every particle of disease is withdrawn from the system. Inordinate itching of the skin is allayed at once by bathing the parts.

For Piles, Wounds, Cuts, Ulcers or Sores, no remedy is so prompt in soothing and healing as Papillon Skin Cure. It does not smart or burn.

Directions in ten languages accompany every bottle.

PAPILLON COUGH CURE

Can be administered to infants without the slightest danger. It does not contain drugs or chemicals, but is a harmless vegetable syrup, very delicious to the taste, that relieves and positively cures **WHOOPING COUGH** at once, and is a permanent cure for Bronchial or Winter Cough, Bronchitis and Pulmonary Catarrh.

The many testimonials received by us, of the efficacy of this medicine, almost permits us to warrant a cure. It is wonderful how promptly it relieves.

Directions in ten languages accompany every bottle.

PAPILLON CATARRH CURE

Cures all diseases of the Nasal Organs, by insufflation, injection or by spraying, in children or adults. Cleanses the nostrils and permits natural breathing.

It is a specific cure for *Cold in the Head*—caused by sudden changes in the atmosphere—Snuffles, Sneezing, Watery Eyes and pain in the Head.

Bronchial Catarrh, Acute or Chronic Catarrh, also Rose Cold, this remedy will permanently cure. It takes the front rank as a cure for Hay Fever, as many testimonials certify. It has been used several years successfully.

The application of this medicine is soothing, not irritating. It does not smart; it is delightful to use.

Directions in ten languages accompany every bottle.

PAPILLON BLOOD CURE

A specific cure for all diseases of the Blood, Liver, Stomach, Bowels and Kidneys. This medicine is absolutely vegetable. It is the prescription of an eminent physician, who has used it in his special practice for thirty years. For all diseases originating in impairment of the blood, as Anæmia, Sick Headache, Nervousness, Female Weaknesses, Liver Complaint, Dyspepsia, Jaundice, Biliousness, and Kidney diseases, this medicine is absolutely sure. This medicine does not contain any mineral, is absolutely vegetable, restores the blood to a healthy condition, regulating excesses and supplying deficiencies, and prevents disease.

Directions in ten languages accompany every bottle.

These Goods are neatly put up in bottles holding ten ounces of medicine, incased in neat cartoons, with full directions in ten languages. The price is uniform for all, one dollar per bottle, six bottles for five dollars. For sale by all Druggists. PAPILLON MANUFACTURING COMPANY, Proprietors.

68 and 70 Wabash Avenue, CHICAGO.

MUTTON AND LAMB.

Note—Mutton should be quite fat, and the fat clear, hard and white; when yellow it is old, and should be rejected. The lean of fat mutton will be juicy and tender, and is of a deep dark red color. The longer it is hung before cooking—provided it is not tainted—the more tender it will be; and if washed with vinegar every day and then thoroughly dried it will keep a long time. During the summer months, if rubbed with ground pepper and ginger it will keep off flies. For roasts, choose the shoulder, loin or haunch, for boiling the leg, and the small ribs for chops. Cuts from the round of the leg are mutton *steaks*, not properly chops, though so termed by some. They are usually tough, and inferior to rib chops for broiling.

133. Boiled Mutton with Caper Sauce—Into a large pot of boiling water put a handful of salt. Select a leg of mutton, with the fat clear, hard and white; wash it and rub salt into every part. If desired rare, cook two hours; if well done, three hours, or even more, according to size. Make a sauce of a pint of hot milk, thickened with flour; add butter, salt, pepper and two tablespoons capers; small chopped pickle will answer the place of capers, if not convenient. A mint sauce similar to that served with roast lamb may be used, if preferred. Serve boiled mutton with hot plates.

134. Leg of Mutton a la Venison—Remove all the rough fat from the mutton and lay it in a deep earthen dish; rub into it thoroughly the following: One tablespoon salt, one each of celery-salt, brown sugar, black pepper, English mustard, allspice, and some sweet herbs, all powdered and mixed; after which pour over it slowly a teacup good vinegar, cover tightly, and set in a cool place four or five days, turning it and basting often with the liquid each day. To cook, put in a kettle a quart of boiling water, place over it an inverted shallow pan, and on it lay the meat just as removed from the pickle; cover the kettle tightly and stew four hours. Do not let the water touch the meat. Add a cup of hot water to the pickle remaining and baste with it. When done, thicken the liquid with flour and strain through a fine sieve, to serve with the meat; also a relish of currant jelly, the same as for venison.

135. Mutton Chops, Broiled—Select good fat chops from the rack of the fore-quarter; cut very thick—to obtain which cut off two ribs, remove the bone from one and press the meat closely to the other; also neatly trim off the meat from the small part of the bone for two or three inches, to serve as a handle. Broil over a brisk charcoal or coke fire upon a wire gridiron, turning frequently until both sides are done to fancy. Serve on a hot platter, and garnish the chops by neatly wrapping around the handle of each clear white paper, and lay a sprig of fresh celery-top on each chop.

136. Mutton Chops, Fried—Rub them with salt and pepper, put in the frying-pan, cover them, and fry five minutes, turning but once; then dip them in well-beaten egg, and then in fine cracker or bread crumbs, and fry until tender or browned nicely on each side.

137. Mutton Chops, Fried—Put them in a dripping-pan in the oven, with a little salted water and pepper; baste frequently, turning them until brown.

138. Haricot of Mutton—If you have left part of a leg of cold boiled mutton, saw off the end of the bone from which the meat has been cut, so as to leave the remainder in a good shape; put both pieces into a closely covered saucepan; cut into dice, a carrot, turnip and onion, put in four cloves and a teaspoon of salt, put in hot water enough to cover the mutton, and simmer gently until the vegetables are very soft; then take out the meat and bone, thicken the gravy with two teaspoons flour wet in cold water. Let it boil up after the meat is removed, and turn it over the mutton.

139. Mutton and Rice—Mince into dice pieces of cold mutton, add a cup of cold boiled rice to one of meat; butter a saucepan well, pour in a little water, add the mutton and rice, and stir until hot, then pour in two eggs slightly beaten, and stir until they are cooked; sprinkle with pepper and salt to taste.

140. Mutton and Tomato Sauce—(See Roast Beef and Tomato Sauce, No. 108); and cook cold roast or boiled mutton as directed for beef.

141. Mutton Pie with Tomatoes—Over the bottom of an earthen baking-dish place a layer of bread crumbs, and over it alternate layers of cold roast mutton cut in thin slices, and tomatoes peeled and sliced, season each with salt, pepper and bits of butter, as laid in. The top layer should be of tomatoes, spread over with bread crumbs. Bake three-quarters of an hour, and serve immediately.

142. Shepherd's Pie—Spread over a small platter, thoroughly buttered, warm mashed potato, mixed with enough milk to make it a little soft, and set in the oven to brown. When stiffened enough, and as brown as pie-crust, pour over it minced cold mutton warmed in a little thickened gravy. Is a fine breakfast dish.

143. Scrambled Mutton—Two cups of chopped cold mutton, two tablespoons hot water, and a piece of butter as large as an English walnut. When the meat is hot, break in three eggs, and constantly stir until the eggs begin to stiffen. Season with pepper and salt.

144. Mutton and Potato Pie—Mince cold mutton with a very little onion, salt and pepper, and put in gravy enough to make it quite moist; also a few capers. Put it into a buttered pudding-dish, and spread the top with mashed potato, and set in the oven. When very hot, rub a piece of butter over the top, and brown in the oven.

Note—Lamb is good at a year old, and is then known as "spring lamb"; early in the season is rather an expensive meat in most locations, and it is quite inferior to good mutton in nutriment, or for digestion.

The meat should be a light red, and fat. If the fore-quarter is not fresh, the large vein will be greenish instead of blue; and if the hindquarter is stale, the kidney fat will have a slight smell.

145. Spring Lamb with Mint Sauce—Select a saddle of a lamb at least a year old, the meat a light red and fat. Rub well with salt and pepper, and roast about an hour and a half, basting frequently with salted water and the drippings. Serve with mint sauce, made as follows: Take fresh young spear-mint leaves stripped from stems, wash and drain them or dry on a cloth, chop very fine, put in a gravy tureen, and to three tablespoons of mint add two of finely-powdered cut-loaf sugar; mix and let it stand a few minutes, then pour over it slowly six tablespoons good cider or white-wine vinegar. The sauce should be made some time before dinner, so that the flavor of the mint may be well extracted.

146. Stewed Lamb with Peas—Take the neck or breast, cut in small pieces, and put in a stewpan with some thinly-sliced salt pork, and enough water to cover it; cover closely and stew until tender, skim off all scum, and add a quart of green shelled peas, adding more water if necessary; cover until the peas are cooked tender, and add a little butter, rolled with flour and pepper to taste; let it simmer a few minutes, and serve.

147. Broiled Breast of Lamb with Cream Sauce—Remove the neck, shoulder and end of the ribs, for an inch and a half, from a fat young spring lamb. Broil over a brisk charcoal or coke fire, frequently turning until done as desired, place on a hot platter, salt, pepper and butter it. Set in the oven while making a sauce as follows: Heat a tablespoon of butter in a small saucepan, add a teaspoon of flour, and stir until perfectly smooth; then add, slowly stirring in, a cup of cold milk, let it boil up once, and season to taste with salt and pepper and a teaspoon of finely chopped fresh parsley. Serve in a gravy boat, all hot.

148. Broiled Lamb Chops—Have them fat and tender from the rack of the forequarter, trim the meat off the small end of the bone about an inch, as a handle, broil over a clear fire, season with pepper and salt and butter, and serve, laying them one over the other, with a slice of lemon on the top one. Garnish the edge of the platter with slices of cucumber and beet pickles, alternately, cut in triangles, the points outwards.

149. Lamb Scallop—One cup each of cold lamb (chopped fine), stewed tomato, and fine bread crumbs. Arrange all in alternate layers in a buttered dish, having the crumbs at top. Season with salt and pepper. Put bits of butter on the top and bake.

150. Lamb a la Matelot—Cut rather thick slices of cold lamb, beat an egg and lay them in it; lift them out one by one; drain for a moment, and then cover with sifted bread crumbs, seasoned with pepper and salt; fry in hot lard

PHILLIPS' HAMS

THEY ARE THE BEST!

WHOLESALE.

PHILLIPS & CO.

23, 25 & 27 North Clinton Street,

CHICAGO.

PORK.

Note—Much care should be taken in the selection of pork. Both fat and lean should be very white, and the skin or rind both smooth and cool to the hand.

151. Stuffed and Roasted Pork—Take a small loin, three tablespoons bread crumbs, one finely-chopped onion, half a teaspoon chopped sage, or summer-savory if preferred, the same of salt and same of pepper, one ounce chopped beef suet, and one tablespoon of drippings. Have each joint of the loin perfectly separated with a cleaver, to carve easily, and make an incision with a knife into the thick part of the meat in which to place the stuffing, which prepare as follows: Mix the bread crumbs with the onions thoroughly, add to this the sage or summer-savory, pepper, salt and suet; when thoroughly mixed press into the incisions made in the pork, and sew together with coarse thread the edges of the meat to keep in the stuffing; grease a stiff sheet of paper with drippings, place the loin into this, securing it with twine; bake in a dry baking-pan, in a quick oven, basting constantly as the grease draws out; allow twenty minutes to the pound, and twenty minutes over. The conventional *apple sauce* may be varied by serving apple fritters (see No. 92 or 93) with this dish, if preferred.

152. Roast Spare-rib—After trimming off the rough ends, crack the ribs through the middle, rub with salt and pepper, fold over where cracked, and stuff same as roast pork (see No. 151), sew up tighly, put in the dripping-pan with a pint of water, with which baste frequently, turning once, so as to bake both sides evenly, until a rich brown.

153. Roast Sucking Pig—One not less than six weeks old, which has been nicely dressed as follows: It should be scored across the back from head to tail, the tail run under the near scores, the ears sewed together by the tips back of the head, the knees bent and run under scores, and before baking, a cracker placed into its mouth. Rub lard all over the surface, and make a stuffiing for it as follows: Take two quarts of corn meal, salted as if for bread, mix to a stiff dough with hot water, put into pan and bake; after it is done, break up and add to it a quarter of a pound of butter, pepper to taste, and also some thyme, sweet marjorum or sage, as fancied. Fill the pig with the stuffing until round and plump, and sew it up; place it on its knees in the pan, which fill with as much water as will be required to baste it frequently until done. Turn while roasting the same as a turkey. Make a gravy of the drippings left in the pan, first straining through a sieve made very hot, and thicken with flour or corn-starch, lastly adding a little hot water, if not sufficient; also sprinkle in a tablespoon of parsley, finely chopped, and a teaspoon of summer savory.

154. Fried Pork Steaks—Fry like beefsteaks, with pepper and salt. If a sausage flavor is liked, sprinkle in a little powdered sage or summer savory.

155. Pork Chops—Are usually fried, but if broiled, trim off most of the fat, and the meat for three inches from the small end, neatly; cook them thoroughly through, turning frequently; put on a hot platter; salt, pepper, and if most of the fat has been removed, butter them. Garnish the platter with sprigs of parsley around the edge.

156. Pork Tenderloins—The tenderloins are unlike any other part of the pork in flavor. They may be either fried or broiled; the latter being dryer, require to be well buttered before serving, which should be done on a hot platter before the butter becomes oily. Fry them in a little lard, turning them to have them cooked through; when done, remove, and keep hot while making a gravy by dredging a little flour into the hot fat; if not enough add a little butter or lard, stir until browned, and add a little milk or cream, stir briskly, and pour over the dish. A little Worcestershire sauce may be added to the gravy if desired.

157. Fried Salt Pork—Cut in thin slices, and freshen in cold milk or milk and water, roll in flour and fry crisp. If required quickly, pour boiling water over the slices, let stand a few minutes, drain and roll in flour as before; drain off most of the grease from the frying-pan; stir in while hot one or two tablespoons flour, about half a pint milk, a little pepper, and salt if over freshened; let it boil, and pour into a gravy dish. A teaspoon of finely-chopped parsley will add pleasantly to the appearance of the gravy.

158. Fried Salt Pork—Cook same as directed for fried tripe (No. 121).

159. Grilled Salt Pork—Take quite thin slices of the thick part of side pork, of a clear white, and thinly streaked with lean; hold one on a toasting fork before a brisk fire to grill; have at hand a dish of cold water, in which immerse it frequently while cooking, to remove the superfluous fat and render it more delicate. Put each slice as cooked in a warm covered pan; when all are done serve hot.

160. Yankee Pork and Beans—Pick over carefully a quart of small white beans, let them soak over night; in the morning wash and drain in another water; put on to boil in cold water with half a teaspoon soda. Boil about thirty minutes; when they are done, the skin of a bean will crack if taken out and blown upon. Drain and put in an earthen pot, first a slice of pork and then the beans, with two or three tablespoons molasses. When all are in, put in the center, half to three-quarters of a pound of well-washed salt pork, with the rind uppermost, and scored across or in squares, season with pepper, and salt if needed, cover all with hot water, and bake six hours or longer in a moderate oven, adding hot water as needed by evaporation, to keep them moist. They cannot be baked too long if this is done. Keep them covered so they will not burn on the top, but remove the cover an hour or so before serving, to brown the top and crisp the pork.

Note—The best hams have a thin skin, with solid fat and a small, short tapering leg or shank, and should weigh from eight to fifteen pounds. Test them by running a steel or knife along the fleshy side close to the bone; if it comes out clean it is good, if smeared it is tainted.

161. Boiled Ham—Take a ham, say of ten to twelve pounds, pour boiling water over it, and let it cool enough to wash and scrape it clean; put it in a perfectly clean boiler, with cold water to cover it; bring it to the boiling point, when place it on the back part of the stove or range to simmer steadily six or seven hours, or until it is tender, when tested with a fork. Be careful to keep the water at a low boiling point, and do not allow it to get much above it. If not suspended in the pot —the better way—the ham should be turned once or twice in the water. When done, place in a large pan to skin; dip the hands in cold water, take the skin between finger and thumb, and pull downward from the knuckle. Set it in a moderate oven, placing the lean side downward; and if you wish it breaded, sift over it powdered crackers, and bake one hour. Baking brings out a great quantity of fat, leaving the meat more delicate, and the ham will keep much longer in warm weather. If before it is used there is a tendency to mould, set it in the oven again for a short time.

162. Broiled Ham—Cut the ham in slices of medium thickness, place on a hot gridiron, and broil until the fat readily flows out and the meat is slightly browned; take it from the gridiron with a knife and fork, and drop into a pan of cold water, then return again to the gridiron; repeat several times, and the ham is done. Place on a hot platter, spread it with sufficient butter, and serve quickly. If the ham is too fat, trim off a part. It is very difficult to broil ham without burning the fat, but this does not impair the flavor. Slices of salt-pork or bacon may also be cooked in same way.

163. Broiled Ham—Shave off from a good, firm ham, several slices of about a quarter inch in thickness; trim off nearly all the fat around the edge; put it on a wire broiler over a brisk charcoal or coke fire, and cook quickly; closely watch, and turn the gridiron whenever it is likely to burn. If cut as directed, a slice will be cooked in three to four minutes, when place it in a hot pan, butter it, and cover. When all are done, arrange the slices neatly upon a hot platter, and serve quickly, with hot plates.

164. Fried Ham and Eggs—Place the slices in boiling water, and cook until tender; put them in a frying-pan to brown, and dish on a platter. Fry some eggs by dipping gravy over them until done, instead of turning. Take up carefully without breaking, and lay upon the slices of hams.

THE

Washington Ice Company

OF CHICAGO,

The Largest Ice Company in the West,

IS ALWAYS PREPARED TO FURNISH

ICE

OF THE BEST QUALITY,

In any desired quantity and at short notice.

Principal Office: 79 Clark St., Chicago.

VEAL.

Veal—The veal of calves from four to six weeks old is the best; if younger it is unwholesome, and if older it is apt to be too lean. The meat should be clear and firm, and the fat white. If dark and thin, it is not good. The hind-quarter is the choicest joint, and is divided into the *loin* and *leg*. The neck or fore-quarter is used for fricassees and stews, and for pies or chops.

165. Roast Loin of Veal—Wash and rub it well with salt and pepper, leaving in the kidney, around which put considerable salt. Roll it up (the ribs having been well cracked), let it stand two hours, and during that time make a stuffing of bread crumbs, moistened with a little hot water and butter, or chopped salt pork if preferred, and also an egg. Unroll the loin, put the stuffing well around the kidney, fold and secure with several coils white cotton twine wound around in all directions; place in the dripping pan with the thick side down, and put in a rather hot oven, graduated after it commences to roast to moderate; in half an hour add a little hot water to the pan, and baste often; in another half hour turn over the roast, and when about done, dredge lightly with flour and baste with melted butter. Before serving carefully remove the twine. A roast of four to five pounds will bake in about two hours. For a gravy, skim off some of the fat if there is too much in the drippings, dredge in some flour, stir until brown, add some hot water if necessary, boil a few minutes, stir in such sweet herbs as fancied, and put in a gravy boat. Serve with green peas and lemon jelly. Is very nice sliced cold for lunch, and Worcestershire or Chili sauce forms a fine relish.

166. Gravy for Roast Veal—Mix one dessertspoon of dry mustard, one teaspoon salt, a quarter ditto of pepper, half teaspoon celery-salt, with one tablespoon of butter. When all are well stirred together, add the yelks of two eggs; beat well and stir into a cup of hot sweet cream; stir all together over a tea-kettle until it thickens like a custard, then take from the fire and add two tablespoons vinegar.

167. Roast Veal Pie—Cut cold roast veal into slices, with the stuffing, and lay in a deep dish, adding pepper and salt; dredge lightly with flour, and put in the gravy that was left and a little hot water added to it. A dish holding three pints will require a cup of gravy. Cover the top with a crust made of one pint flour with two teaspoons baking powder sifted through it, add a piece of butter half the size of an egg, rubbing into the flour with the hand; wet with sweet milk enough to make a dough as soft as can be handled. When made, score the crust in the center; put it over the dish, and bake in a brisk oven. Serve in the dish in which it is baked, set upon a round soup or cake plate.

168. Veal Cutlets—Fry the cutlets brown in sweet lard or beef drippings; dip in a batter made of half a pint of milk, a well-beaten egg and flour, and fry again; also drop spoonfuls of the batter in the lard after the veal is taken up; take them out to serve on top of the meat; put a little flour paste in the gravy with salt and pepper, let it come to a boil, and pour over the whole. The veal should be cut thin, pounded, and cooked nearly an hour.

169. Veal Stew—Boil two pounds and a half of the breast of veal one hour in water enough to cover, add a dozen potatoes, and cook half an hour; before taking off the stove add a pint of milk and flour enough to thicken; season to taste.

170. Ragout of Veal—Cut cold veal cutlets into small pieces; put a piece of butter as large as a walnut in a frying-pan, and when hot, drop in the veal and stir a few minutes; dredge in a little flour, and then pour in a cup of stock made by boiling the bone and dry bits of veal; season with salt and pepper, and let it boil up; then add four cold, boiled potatoes cut in slices; rub the platter with a clove of garlic, and pour the ragout on it.

171. Veal Pot Pie—Put two or three pounds of veal—that from the loin or breast is best, but other parts may be used—cut in a dozen pieces, and put into a quart of cold water; make a quart of soda biscuit dough, take two thirds of it, roll a quarter inch thick; cut into strips an inch wide by three long; pare and slice six potatoes; boil the veal until tender, and take out all the bone, leaving three or four pieces, put in two handsful potatoes and several strips of dough, then add veal and dough, seasoning with salt and pepper, and a little butter, until all the veal is in the pot; add boiling water enough to cover; make a crust out of the remaining dough, slit the center to let steam escape, and place over the whole. Put on a tight lid and boil gently twenty or thirty minutes without uncovering.

172. Veal with Oysters—Cut two pounds tender veal into thin bits, dredge with flour, and fry in sufficient hot lard to prevent sticking. When nearly done, add a pint and a half fine oysters; thicken with flour, season with salt and pepper, and cook until done. Serve in a covered dish, hot.

173. Veal Toast—One cup chopped veal, one cup hot water, a piece of butter as large as a butternut, one teaspoon salt, and one-fourth teaspoon pepper; have ready on a platter slices of bread nicely toasted brown, and buttered; if the crusts are hard, dip the edges in hot water; when the minced veal is quite hot, pour it on the toast.

174. Cold Veal and Tomatoes—Arrange delicate slices of cold roast veal on a platter, put over them peeled and sliced raw tomatoes, and pour over the dish a salad dressing made as follows: Rub to a powder with a silver spoon the yelks of two hard-boiled eggs, add half a teaspoon salt and the same each of pepper, white sugar and **dry** English mustard. When these are all well mixed with the egg, add two tablespoons of best salad oil, stirring in gradually, and when well mixed put in half a cup of vinegar. All should be very cold, and so kept until served.

175. Veal Patties—Cut portions of the neck or breast of veal into small pieces, and, with a little salt pork cut fine, stew gently for ten or fifteen minutes; season with pepper and salt and a small piece of celery chopped coarsely, also of the yellow top, picked (not chopped) up; stir in a paste made of a tablespoon flour, the yelk of one egg, and milk to make a thin batter; let all come to a boil, and it is ready for the patties. Make the patties of a light, flaky crust, as for tarts; cut round, the size of a small sauceplate; the center of each, for about three inches, cut half way through, to be raised and serve as a cover. Put a spoonful of the stew in each crust, lay on it the top, and serve. Stewed oysters or lamb may be used in place of veal.

176. Sweetbreads—There are two in a calf, which are considered delicacies. Select the largest. The color should be clear and a shade darker than the fat. Before cooking in any manner let them lie for half an hour in tepid water; then throw into hot water to whiten and harden, after which draw off the outer casing, remove the little pipes, and cut into thin slices. They should always be thoroughly cooked.

177. Broiled Sweetbreads—After preparing as above, spread plenty of butter over them, and broil on a fine wire gridiron over hot charcoals, turning often.

178. Fried Sweetbreads—Parboil five minutes, wipe dry, lard them with narrow strips of fat salt pork with a larding needle, taking deep, long stitches, or they will break out. Put a very little butter or lard in a frying-pan, and lay in the sweetbreads when hot; fry to a crisp brown, turning them often.

179. Fricasseed Sweetbreads—If they are uncooked, cut into thin slices, let them simmer in a rich gravy for three-quarters of an hour, add a well-beaten egg, two tablespoons cream and a tablespoon chopped parsley; stir all together for a few minutes and serve immediately.

180. Sweetbreads with Green Peas—Lard five sweetbreads as above directed, letting the strips of pork project half an inch evenly on the upper side, put in a saucepan with half a pint water, and let stew slowly for half an hour; take out and put in a small dripping-pan, with a little butter and a sprinkling of flour, brown slightly, add half a gill of mingled milk and water, season with pepper; heat a half pint cream and stir it in the gravy in the pan. Have the peas ready boiled and seasoned, place the sweetbreads in the center of the dish, pour the gravy over them, and put the peas around them.

WHOLESALE AND RETAIL DEALERS IN

Hard and Soft
⟹COAL⟸

MAIN OFFICE:

97 E. Washington Street,

CHICAGO.

TELEPHONE No. 5039.

POULTRY AND GAME.

181. Baked Chicken—Split them lengthwise, soak half an hour in cold water, wipe perfectly dry, and put in a dripping-pan, bone side down, without any water; if the oven is hot and the chickens young, should be done in half an hour. Take out and season with salt, pepper and butter; place one above another closely, and place in a pan of boiling water, covering them closely to keep them moist until served; meantime boil the giblets in a little water, and after the chickens are taken out of the dripping-pan, pour in the giblet water; thicken it, and having chopped the giblets, add them to it, making the gravy to serve with chickens. Is fully equal to broiled chicken.

182. Baked Chicken with Parsnips—Wash, scrape and quarter a few parsnips; parboil for twenty minutes; prepare a young chicken by splitting open at back; place in a dripping-pan, the skin side up, lay parsnips around the chicken, sprinkle with salt and pepper, and add an egg-sized lump of butter, or two or three slices nice pickled pork; put enough water in the pan to prevent burning, place in oven and bake until both chickens and parsnips are done a delicate brown. Serve the chicken separately on a platter, pouring the gravy in the pan over the parsnips.

183. Boiled Chicken—A pair are usually boiled. Dress and truss with wooden skewers, or tie the legs with twine; stuff with a stuffing made of bread and butter moistened with milk, flavor with a little parsley or summer-savory; suspend them in a pot to boil an hour, or until done. Make an egg sauce sprinkled with chopped parsley to serve with it. Also serve a slice of boiled bacon, ham or salt pork to each plate at table.

184. To Broil Chicken or Quails—Cut the bird open in the back; lay on the meat board until it will lay flat; put on a gridiron over a good bed of coals, and broil until a nice brown, but do not burn. It will take twenty or thirty minutes to cook thoroughly, and will do so much better if covered with a pie-tin held down by a weight, so that it will lie close to the gridiron. While it is broiling, put the giblets in a stewpan, and boil in a pint of water until tender; chop fine, and add flour, butter, salt and pepper; also stir in a cup of sweet cream. When done, dip birds in this gravy, and let boil for half a minute; send to table quite hot.

185. Fried Spring Chicken—Put in the frying-pan on the stove about half a tablespoon each of lard and butter; when hot, lay in the chicken cut open on the back, and sprinkle with flour, salt and pepper; cover over and cook over a moderate fire; when a light brown turn it over and again sprinkle with flour, salt and pepper; if necessary add more lard and butter, and cook slowly until done; make a gravy as for baked chicken in No. 181; or, the following is a rich and very nice gravy without cream: Take the yelk of an egg, beat up light, strain and stir slowly into the gravy after the flour and milk have been stirred in and thoroughly cooked; as soon as it boils up it is done.

186. Fricasseed Chicken—Cut up and put on to boil, skin side down, in a small quantity of water; season with pepper and salt, also slices of onion if liked; stew gently until tender; remove the chicken, and add half a pint of milk or cream to the gravy; thicken with butter and flour rubbed smoothly together in a little of the gravy; let it boil a few minutes; add a little chopped parsley, and serve. A few slices of clear white celery from the bottom of the stalk may be added, if that flavor is liked.

187. Fricasseed Chicken—Put the chicken cut up, in a sauce pan with barely enough water to cover it, stew gently until tender; have a frying-pan prepared with a few slices of salt pork; drain the chicken and fry with pork until a rich brown; then take out of the pan and put in the broth in which the chicken was stewed, thicken with browned flour mixed smooth with a little water, and season with pepper. Put the chicken and pork back in the gravy, let it simmer a few minutes, and serve very hot.

188. Chicken Lunch for Traveling—Cut a young chicken down the back; wash and wipe dry; season with salt and pepper; put in a dripping-pan, and bake in a moderate oven three-quarters of an hour. This is much better for traveling lunch than when seasoned with butter.

189. Chicken Pie—Cut up two young chickens, in hot water enough to cover them, and as the water boils out add more, so as to have enough for the pie, and also for a gravy to serve with it; boil until tender; line the sides of a four or six-quart pan with a rich baking powder or soda-biscuit dough a quarter inch thick, put in part of the chicken, season with salt, pepper and butter, lay on a few thin strips or squares of dough, add the rest of the chicken and season as before; five or six fresh eggs beaten, or a few new potatoes in their season, may be also added. Take the liquor in which the chicken was boiled, with butter, salt and pepper, add a part of it to the pie, and cover with the crust rolled a quarter inch thick, with a hole in the center the size of a tea-cup. Keep adding the broth as needed, and plentiful, as there cannot be too much of the gravy. Bake about an hour in a moderate oven. If the flavor of celery is liked, a few inside layers or slices of the bottom of the stalk may be put in with the strips of dough. In that case, garnish the top of the pie with small, bright celery leaves, neatly arranged in a circle.

190. Chicken Pot Pie—Take two young chickens, joint and cut up; then prepare and cook as directed for VEAL POT PIE. See No. 171.

191. Chicken Puree—Pick into small bits, cold roast or boiled chicken; season with salt and pepper. Boil the bones and skin in enough water to cover; strain and return to the fire. When it boils, stir in for each cupful of the stock a small teaspoon flour rubbed in one teaspoon butter; add a little celery-salt, and stir in the meat. Serve with small triangles of bread previously fried crisp in very hot lard.

192. Salmi of Chicken—Cut cold chicken into small bits, and heat in enough drawn butter to make it quite moist; season with pepper and celery-salt; when hot take from the fire, add a well-beaten egg and a teaspoon lemon juice. Cover the bottom of a covered dish with bread crumbs and pour in the chicken; sift crumbs over the top, stick bits of butter over it, and bake until brown. The gravy left from the chicken can be used instead of the drawn butter if desired.

193. Chicken and Oyster Croquettes—Take one cup cold chicken chopped very fine, one saucerful of cold scalloped oysters, also chopped; half a cup sifted bread crumbs, pepper, salt and a little mace, one egg beaten lightly; add a little broth made of the bones of the chicken, boiled in just water enough to cover them. Have the mixture as soft as can be handled (an experienced cook can handle it much softer than a novice). Form into long rolls as large as a finger; roll in sifted crumbs and fry in very hot lard. Serve with slices of lemon.

194. Chicken Salad without Celery—Cut cold chicken in small bits, or tear it into shreds; mix with it an equal quantity of nice raw cabbage chopped fine; season with pepper and celery salt. Prepare a dressing by beating the yelks of four eggs; add to these half a cup butter, half a cup cream, half a gill vinegar, and one heaping spoon prepared mustard; put this mixture into a bowl over a tea-kettle, or in a hot pan of water; stir until it is thicker than boiled custard, and take from the fire. Take part of the dressing and thin it with vinegar until it can be easily mixed with the chicken and cabbage. Pour over the top the remainder of the dressing. Some like a little sugar in the dressing.

195. Roast Turkey with Oyster Stuffing—Dress and rub the turkey well, inside and out, with salt and pepper; truss or twine it; put in a steamer and steam two hours, or until it begins to grow tender, lifting the cover occasionally and sprinkling lightly with salt; then take out, loosen the legs, and rub the inside again with salt and pepper. Make the stuffing as follows: Take a loaf of stale bread, cut off the crust and soften it in a pan with boiling water; drain off immediately and cover closely; crumble the soft part of the bread very fine, and add a half pound of melted butter, or more if to be very rich, and a teaspoon each of salt and pepper, or enough to season rather highly. Drain off the liquor from a quart of nice oysters, bring to a boil, skim and pour over the bread crumbs, adding the soaked crust and one or two eggs; mix all thoroughly with the hands, and if too dry, moisten with a little milk; lastly, add the oysters, being careful not to break them; or first put in a spoonful of stuffing and then three or four oysters, and so on until the turkey is filled, stuffing the breast first. Flour a small cloth and place over the openings, tying down with twine; spread the turkey all over with butter, salt and pepper; place in a dripping-pan in a well heated oven; add half a pint water, and roast two hours, basting often with a little water, butter, salt and pepper, kept warm in tin placed on the back of the stove. A swab is better than a spoon to baste with. Turn until nicely browned on all sides, and about half an hour before it is done, baste with butter alone and dredge with a little flour, which will give the turkey a frothy appearance. When the turkey is dished, if there is much fat in the pan, pour off most of it and add the giblets, together with the water in which they have previously been cooked until tender, now stewed down to about a pint; place one or two heaping tablespoons flour (half of it browned flour) in a pint bowl, mix smooth in a little cream or milk, and add to the gravy in the pan; boil several minutes, constantly stirring and pour into a gravy tureen. Serve with currant or apple jelly. This is an excellent way to cook a large turkey; while, from being steamed, it does not make so good an appearance at table, it will prove very tender and palatable.

196. Roast Turkey, English Style—Kill several days before cooking, and let it hang by the legs until used. Prepare in the usual manner; stuff with bread crumbs—rejecting the crust—rubbed fine, moistened with butter and two eggs, and seasoned with salt, pepper, parsley, sage and sweet marjoram; sew up, truss and place to roast in a rack within a dripping-pan; spread with bits of butter, turn it and baste frequently with butter, pepper, salt and water; a few minutes before it is done glaze over with the white of an egg; take up the turkey, pour off most of the fat, add the chopped giblets and the water in which they were boiled, which thicken with flour and butter rubbed together; stir all in the dripping pan, let it boil once well, and serve in a gravy boat. Serve with celery-sauce and stewed gooseberries. Garnish with fried oysters. Select a turkey of eight to ten pounds. If in roasting it is likely to brown too much, cover with a white paper, buttered.

197. Boned Turkey—With a sharp knife slit the skin down the back, and raising one side at a time with the fingers, separate the flesh from the bones with a knife until the wings and legs are reached. These unjoint from the body, and cutting through to the bone, turn back the flesh and remove the bones. When the bones are removed the flesh may be reshaped by stuffing. Some leave the bones in the wings and legs, as they are quite difficult to remove. Stuff with a forcemeat made of cold lamb or veal, and a little pork chopped fine and seasoned with salt, pepper, sage or savory, and the juice of one lemon; sew into shape, turn the ends of the wings under, and press the legs close to the back, and tie all firmly, so that the upper surface may be plump and smooth for the carver. Lard with two or three rows on the top; bake until thoroughly done, basting often with salt and water and a little butter. This is a difficult dish to attempt by any but skillful cooks. Carve across in slices, and serve with tomato sauce.

198. Boiled Turkey Stuffed with Oysters—Wash it thoroughly and rub salt through it; fill with a stuffing of bread and butter, moistened with milk and seasoned with sage, salt and pepper, mixed with a pint raw oysters; tie the legs and wings close to the body, place in salted boiling water with the breast downward; skim often; boil about two hours, but not till the skin breaks; serve with oyster sauce. Boil a piece of nicely-pickled salt pork, and serve at table a thin slice to each plate. Some use bacon or ham instead of pork.

199. Roast Goose—The goose should not be more than eight months old, and the fatter the more tender and juicy the meat. A " green goose," about four months old, is the choicest. Kill at least twenty-four hours before cooking; dress and stuff; prepare a gravy as directed for roast duck, tame or wild (see No. 212.) Bake two hours or more. If an old goose it will have red and hairy legs, and should be par-boiled; if too old, is unfit for the table.

200. Deviled Goose—Take the legs and wings of cold roast goose; broil them on a gridiron until heated through; have ready a little butter, pepper, salt and English mustard, and one tablespoon sharp wine or cider vinegar, all mixed together. Turn this over the goose and serve hot.

201. Roast Duck—(See Roast Duck, Tame or Wild, No. 212.)

202. A Stuffing for Ducks, Chickens or Beef—Prepare some boiled and mashed potatoes, as if for the table; except they should be rather dryer, stuff the chickens (or a roast of beef) with this, and bake them as usual. For ducks add finely chopped onion. If a bread dressing is also desired, it may be cooked in the corner of the pan.

203. Boiled Duck—Dress and rub inside with salt and pepper; truss and tie in shape, drawing the legs into the body, in which put one or two leaves of sage, a little finely-chopped onion and a little jellied stock or gravy; rub over with salt and pepper; make a paste in the proportion of one-half pound of butter to one pound of flour, in which enclose the duck; tie a cloth around all, and boil two hours or until quite tender, keeping it well covered with boiling water. Make a brown gravy, as follows: Put an egg-sized lump of butter in a sauce-pan, with a little minced onion; cook until slightly brown, and add a small tablespoon flour; stir well, and when quite brown add a half pint of stock or water. Let cook a few minutes, strain and add the chopped giblets which have been previously stewed tender.

204. Duck Pie—Cut all the meat from cold roast ducks; put the bones and stuffing into cold water; cover them and let boil; put the meat into a deep dish, pour on enough of the stock made from the bones to moisten; cover with pastry slit in the center with a knife and bake a light brown.

205. Deviled Turkey—Cut gashes in the legs and upper joints of cold roast turkey, and rub in pepper, salt and mustard (some use curry powder also); heat them through on a gridiron. Serve very hot.

GAME.

Note.—The rule for cooking is for all white-meated game to be cooked *well done*, and dark-meated, under done or rare. The general taste will, however, require all to be well cooked. The keeping of game hanging for some time will make it more tender, and bring out the flavor so highly appreciated by the epicure, but not so well favored by a majority of the community.

206. Venison—When young, the fat is thick, clear and close, and the meat a reddish brown. It first begins to taint near the haunches; test by running in a knife or steel; if tainted, there will be a rank smell and a greenish appearance. It may, however, be kept a long time by the following process: Wash it well in milk and water, and dry perfectly with a cloth; then dust ground black pepper over every part. The flesh of the doe about four years old is the sweetest and best. Either the haunch, neck, shoulder or saddle should be roasted, the breast broiled, and fry or broil the steaks with salt pork. Being a rather lean meat, roasts require much larding. The steaks require more cooking than for beef.

207. Saddle of Venison—Use a saddle of venison of about ten pounds. Cut some salt pork in strips about two inches long and an eighth of an inch thick, with which lard the saddle, with two rows on each side. In a large dripping-pan cut two carrots, one onion, and some salt pork in thin slices; add two bay leaves, two cloves, four kernels of allspice, half a lemon, sliced, and season with salt and pepper; place the saddle of venison in the pan, with a quart of good stock and a small piece of butter, and let it boil about fifteen minutes on top of the stove; then put it in a hot oven and bake, basting well every five minutes, until it is medium rare, so that the blood runs when cut; serve with jelly or a wine sauce. If the venison is desired well done, cook much longer, and use a cream sauce with it.—*Grand Pacific Hotel, Chicago.*

208. Roast Haunch of Venison—Wash in warm water and dry with a cloth; butter a sheet of white paper and put over the fat; lay it in a deep baking-dish, with a very little hot water; cover with a close-fitting lid or with a coarse paste half an inch thick, smeared evenly over the top; if the latter is used, lay over it one or two sheets of coarse paper. Cook in a moderate oven for three to four hours, according to the size of the haunch; about twenty minutes before it is done quicken the fire a little, remove the dish cover (or paper and paste), dredge with flour, and baste well with butter until nicely frothed and of a delicate brown; garnish the knuckle bone with a frill of white paper, and serve with a gravy made from its own drippings, the platter and plates very hot. Currant jelly is the conventional relish with roast venison.

209. Roast Wild Goose—As a rule wild geese have a strong or fishy flavor, and are inferior to wild duck. If you have one, however, dress and cook same as for tame roast goose (No. 199).

210. Wild Ducks—There are many varieties of ducks peculiar to different sections, of which the canvas-back, mallard, teal, and at the South the red-head, are leading favorites. Young ducks are tender under the wings and have transparent webs; wild ducks have reddish legs, and tame ones yellow. If wild ducks are fishy, they should be scalded in salt and water before washing, and if old, they should be parboiled.

212. Roast Duck (Tame or Wild)—Cut the neck close to the back, beat the breast-bone flat with a rolling-pin, tie the wings and legs securely, and stuff with the following: Three pints bread crumbs, six ounces butter, or part butter and salt pork, two chopped onions and one teaspoon each of sage, black pepper and salt. Do not stuff very full, and sew up the openings firmly to keep the flavor in and the fat out. If not fat enough it should be larded with salt pork or tie a slice upon the breast. Place in a baking-pan, with a little water, and baste frequently with salt and water—some add onion and some vinegar—turn often, so that the sides and back may all be nicely browned. When nearly done, baste with butter and a little flour. These directions will apply to tame geese as well as ducks. Young ducks should roast from twenty-five to thirty minutes, and full-grown ones for an hour or more, with frequent basting. If quite old, parboil a few minutes before roasting. Some prefer them underdone, but served very hot; but, as a rule, thorough cooking will prove more palatable. Serve with currant jelly or apple sauce and green peas.

213. Game Pie—Family Style (For 10 persons)—Clean well inside and out, about two dozen small birds—quail, snipe, woodcock, etc.—and split them in half; put them in a saucepan, with some soup stock or beef broth, if you have it; if not, use a gallon of cold water; put over a hot fire, and when it boils skim off all scum that rises; then add a little salt, pepper, ground cloves, mace, one bay leaf, two small carrots, and one onion, with three cloves stuck in it. Add half a pound of salt pork cut into dice, and let all boil until tender; use care that there be enough broth to cover the birds.

Put in another saucepan a quarter pound of butter, with two tablespoons browned flour; mix it well, and stir it into a part of the broth or gravy, making a thin sauce; strain off the rest of the broth, and remove the vegetables and spices, which add to the sauce. Cut some potatoes into small dice, about the same quantity as meat, and put all into a deep dish or bowl; cover with a paste or dough, and bake slowly. The baking may be done in small vegetable dishes, forming a pie for each person.—*Grand Pacific Hotel, Chicago.*

214. Roast Prairie Chicken or Pheasant—Carefully cut out all the shot, wash thoroughly but quickly, using some soda in the water, rinse and dry; stuff, sew up and tie down, or skewer through the legs and wings. Place in a steamer over hot water until tender, then remove to a dripping-pan, cover with butter, sprinkle with salt and pepper, dredge with flour, place in the oven, and baste with melted butter until a nice brown. Serve with either apple-sauce, cranberries or currant jelly.

215. Broiled Pheasant or Prairie Chicken—Scald and skin, cut off the breast, and the rest up in joints, being careful to remove all shot; put in hot water, all except the breast, and boil until it can be easily pierced with a fork; take out, rub over with salt, pepper and butter, and broil with the breast over a brisk fire; take out, place a lump of butter on each piece, and set all in the oven a few minutes.

Squirrels may be prepared in this manner, but with no separation of the meat.

216. Roast Quails—Pluck and dress like chicken, wipe clean, and rub both inside and out with salt and pepper; stuff with any of the stuffings fancied for poultry or game, and sew up; spread them with butter, and place in a hot oven with a good, steady heat, turning and basting often with hot salted water, butter and pepper. Bake three-quarters of an hour. When about half done, add a little hot water to the pan, and also place another dripping-pan over them to prevent browning too much; add to the gravy in the pan flour and butter rubbed together, and water if needed.

217. Quail on Toast—Dry, pick and singe them with paper; cut off the head, and the legs at first joint; draw and split them down the back; soak in salted water for five or ten minutes; drain and dry with a cloth; lard them with bacon or butter, and rub salt over them; place on a broiler and turn often, dipping two or three times into melted butter; broil about twenty minutes. Have ready as many slices of nicely buttered toast as there are birds, and place one on each slice, breast upwards. All should go to table hot and with hot plates.

218. Reed Birds—Roast before an open fire, suspended by a wire or string, and kept turning (or, put in a row on a skewer and use an English bottle-jack), let drip in a pan, basting. This is the Southern method and the best. Or, they may be boiled in a crust like dumplings.

219. Reed Birds Au Pomme de Terre—Wash and peel very thinly quite large potatoes of equal size; cut a deep slice off one end of each, and scoop out a hole large enough to contain a bird; drop a bit of butter into each bird, with pepper and salt, and put one into the hole of each potato, putting on as covers the slices cut off; clip off the other end so they will stand upright. When so arranged set in a baking pan with a little water to prevent burning; bake slowly and serve in the same dish.

220. Snipe—Are best roasted with a piece of salt pork tied on to the breast; or, they may be stuffed and baked like quail; or, broiled same as woodcock.

221. Woodcock—Of all game birds this outranks in tenderness and delicacy of flavor, the thigh being the tidbit.

To Broil—Split them through the back, basting with butter, and serve on toast, the beak under the wing.

To Roast—Split them, place in a Dutch oven before an open fire, and bake for fifteen or twenty minutes, as fancied, under or well done.

222. Fried Woodcock—Dress, wipe clean; tie the legs; skin the head and neck; turn the beak under the wing and tie it; tie a piece of bacon over it, and immerse in boiling fat two or three minutes. Serve on browned toast, nicely trimmed and buttered.

223. Squirrels—There are many species common to this country, among them the black, red, gray and fox. Gophers and chipmunks may also be classed as another, but smaller variety. They should be carefully skinned and laid in salt water a short time before cooking; if old, should be parboiled. They are fine when broiled, the hind quarters being the choicest parts, unless when in the fall they are fat and full breasted. Are excellent cooked in any other way, with thin slices of pork. They are also delicious when made into a pie, like Veal or Chicken.

224. Rabbits—They are in the best condition in mid-winter, and may be fricasseed, like chicken, in white or brown sauce, or made like a chicken pie.

225. Roast Rabbits—Stuff with a stuffing made of bread crumbs, chopped salt pork, thyme, onion, pepper and salt; sew up; rub over with a little butter, or secure in it a few slices salt pork; add some water in the pan, and baste often. Serve mashed potatoes and currant jelly with it.

226. Pigeons—Should be cooked a long time, as they are usually quite lean and tough, except the squabs or young ones, and are better to lie in salt water half an hour before cooking; if old, parboil. Are nice roasted, or made into a pie, or the breast broiled.

227. Pigeon Pot Pie—Prepare and cook same as Veal Pot-pie. See No. 171.

228. Compote of Pigeons (For 10 persons)—Use one dozen dressed pigeons. Cut up some vegetables very thin, and put in a roasting pan with thin rashers of salt pork and some spices; lay in the pigeons, breast upwards, and sprinkle them with salt and pepper; bake in a hot oven, turning them over once or twice, until a nice brown; dredge with a little flour, and brown again. Remove the pigeons to a stewpan, and strain the gravy, to add to the pigeons; if not sufficient, use some beef broth, to make enough to cover them, and cook until done; then cut some salt pork in small strips, fry them well in a pan, and drain off the fat; add the pork to the pigeons, and serve on toast.—*Grand Pacific Hotel, Chicago.*

229. Broiled Plover—Split through the back and broil over a hot fire, basting frequently with butter. When done, place a bit of butter on each piece, and set in the oven a few minutes to brown. Serve on pieces of buttered toast, with currant jelly.

A HINT TO SPORTSMEN.—To those who may wish to keep prairie chickens, pheasants or other game birds in very hot weather, or to ship long distances, it may prove of value to learn the best manner of doing so. Draw the birds as soon as killed; force down the throat two or three whole peppers, tying a string around just above them; sprinkle inside a little powdered charcoal, and fill the cavity of the body with *very dry* grass—green or wet grass, being heating, will hasten decay. If birds are to be shipped *without* drawing, force a piece of charcoal into the vent, tie a string close around the neck to exclude the air, and make a loop in the string to hang up by. Thus prepared, will bear shipment a long distance.

THE

HEATH & MILLIGAN
"Best" Prepared Paints

(READY FOR USE).

The subject of successfully ornamenting our houses by using divers colored paints on the same building having during the past three years become a study, we, in order to meet the demand, have added to our "BEST" PREPARED PAINTS one tint after another, until now we manufacture seventy-five distinct, beautiful, rich and attractive shades. This spring we have brought out some rare tints which are very fashionable, and which are exceedingly tasty and pleasing. From this variety of tints one cannot fail to make a suitable and satisfactory selection, and to be able to make an almost endless number of effective and harmonious combinations. As to the quality of our goods, we would say they are made from pure material, and we guarantee them to cover as much surface as Strictly Pure White Lead and Linseed Oil; to impart a much finer and more beautiful finish, and to greatly surpass it in durability. They wear without cracking, chalking or peeling off, and weather exposure has but little effect upon them. They give universal satisfaction, and are commended by all who have used them.

Ask your Local Dealers for Sample Cards, and Prices. Should they not have them at hand, do not be put off with any substitute, but persuade your Merchant to send for what you want; failing in this, direct Communication with our House will insure a prompt response.

HEATH & MILLIGAN MFG. CO.
170–174 Randolph St., Chicago, Ill.

FISH.

Note.—When fish are fresh, the eyes are full and bright, the gills a fine, clear red, the body stiff, and the smell not unpleasant. The flavor and excellence of salmon is especially dependent on its freshness: Mackerel should be freshly caught, or are nearly worthless. Nearly all the larger fish are usually boiled, the medium-sized baked or boiled, and smaller kinds fried. The very large ones, as cod, halibut, etc., are cut in steaks or slices for frying or broiling. The heads of some fish, as the cod, halibut, etc. are considered tidbits by many. Brook-trout and smelts should be served with the heads, and most other pan-fish, without. As regards others, the heads are cooked and served simply for appearance, it being a matter of fancy whether they are served or not. Fish is less nutritious than meats, salmon excepted, which is very hearty. The white kinds are least nutritious, and the oily kinds the more difficult of digestion. All fish should be well done and served quite hot.

230. Boiled Fish—*General Directions*—For this purpose a regular *fish-kettle* is very convenient. It is of oblong form, occupying the place of two holes on a stove or range, and contains a perforated tin rack or plate, with a long handle at each end, and resting on the feet a few inches above the bottom. On this the fish rests when boiling, and upon which it is lifted out when done, to avoid breaking. In lieu of a fish kettle, wrap the fish in a cloth, with which it may be gently lifted from the kettle when done. Steaming fish is far superior to boiling, in which case a rack similar to the one above described may be fitted to an ordinary wash boiler; have the holes the size of a five-cent piece. In boiling, the addition of salt and vinegar to the water pleasantly seasons the fish, and hardens the water, so that less of the nutriment is extracted. Always have the water boiling hot when first put in, and then set where it will simmer gently until done; the rule is to allow five to ten minutes to the pound, according to thickness. In boiling salmon, put into tepid water only, in order to preserve its fine color, increasing it to the boiling point, and then boil gently until done. To test, pass a knife along a bone, and if done, it will separate readily. Do not prod it with a fork. All fish should be boiled, steamed or baked in the position, as nearly as possible, that it assumes when in the water. To effect this, place the fish on its belly, and bend the head and tail in opposite directions, thus, (S). To keep it in position, tie a stout cord around the tail, pass it through the body, and tie to the head.
) Fill the fish with a nicely prepared stuffing of rolled cracker or stale bread crumbs, seasoned with butter, pepper, salt, sage, and any other aromatic herbs fancied; sew up; wrap in a well floured cloth tied closely with twine, and boil or steam. The garnishes for boiled fish are: For turbot, fried smelts; for other boiled fish, parsley, sliced

beets, lobster coral, or sliced boiled egg. Do not use the knives, spoons, etc., that are used in cooking fish, for other food, or they will be apt to impart a fishy flavor.

231. Steamed Fish—Secure the tail of the fish in its mouth, the body in a circle; pour over it half a pint of vinegar, seasoned with pepper and salt; let it stand an hour in a cool place; pour off the vinegar, and put it in a steamer over boiling water, and steam twenty minutes, or longer for large fish. When the meat easily separates from the bone it is done. Drain well, and serve on a very clean white napkin, neatly folded and placed on the platter; decorate the napkin around the fish with sprigs of curled parsley, or with fanciful beet cuttings, or alternately with both.

232. Boiled Fresh Cod—Put the fish in a fish-kettle, or proceed as above, and place in boiling water with some salt and scraped horse-radish; let it simmer until done. Place a folded napkin on a platter, turn the fish upon it, and serve with drawn butter, oyster or egg sauce.

233. Boiled Codfish—Soak in a pan of water over night, and simmer two or three hours, or until well done. Serve with drawn butter, with hard boiled egg chopped fine and stirred in; also garnish the fish with slices of hard boiled egg laid on it or around the edge.

234. Broiled Codfish—Fresh codfish steaks are excellent broiled. After soaking sufficiently, grease the bars of the gridiron, broil well, but do not burn. Serve with bits of butter dropped over it, and garnish with fanciful pieces of sliced pickled beet, drained, and placed around the edge of the platter.

235. Codfish a la Mode—Pick up a teacup of salt codfish very fine, and freshen—the desiccated is nice to use—two cups mashed potatoes, one pint cream or milk, two well beaten eggs, half a cup butter, salt and pepper; mix; bake in an earthen baking dish from twenty to twenty-five minutes; serve in same dish, placed on a small platter, covered with a fine napkin.

236. Stewed Codfish—Select a thick and very white codfish, or use the desiccated; pick in small pieces, and put in cold water to freshen; if desired soon, pour off and change the water frequently, but be sure and not get it too fresh. When properly freshened, put it in a stewpan, with one to three cups of warm water, according to quantity; let it stew slowly, and not boil, for half an hour; then add a cup of milk thickened with flour, stew ten minutes longer, and just before serving, stir in one or two well beaten eggs. A nice breakfast dish with hot baked potatoes.

237. Picked Codfish—Pick the fish in fine pieces, and soak in cold water until sufficiently freshened; then drain it well, and add milk enough to cover it. When well scalded, thicken with flour or cornstarch; season with pepper. When taken from the fire, add two eggs, well beaten, make a nice moist paste, and pour the fish over it, or serve plain if preferred.

238. Minced Cod—Flake up cold baked or boiled cod, and to three cups of fish add one of mashed potatoes, a lump of butter the size of a filbert, half a teaspoon corn-starch, and one beaten egg; heat all together, adding the egg last.

239. Cod au Fromage—Of cold boiled macaroni, cut up in short bits, take a cupful, and one of cold boiled cod; mix together; put it in a buttered dish, and lay bits of butter over it; season with salt and pepper, and moisten with cold drawn butter, if you have it; if not, use milk; cover with fine bread crumbs, and sprinkle two tablespoons grated cheese on top; bake until brown, and serve in the baking-dish.

240. Codfish Balls—Soak codfish, cut in small pieces, about an hour in lukewarm water; remove the skin and bones; pick up very fine; put it in cold water and place on the stove; when it boils, change the water and let boil again. Have ready some boiled potatoes, mash and season with butter. While both are hot, put half the codfish with the potatoes; mix in a well beaten egg, and mould into round balls or thick cakes; then fry them in hot lard or drippings, or drop them, like doughnuts, in hot fat enough to float, and skim out. By reheating them, cold potatoes may be used, in which case add a little cream, or milk and butter, and mix while hot.

241. Baked Salmon, Trout or Pickerel—Carefully clean and wipe the fish, and lay in a dripping-pan, with enough hot water to prevent scorching. A perforated sheet of tin, fitting loosely, or several muffin rings, may be used to keep it off the bottom. Lay it in a circle on its belly, head and tail touching, and tied, or as directed in note on fish, bake slowly, basting often with butter and water. When done, have ready a cup of sweet cream to which a few spoons of hot water have been added; stir in two large spoons of melted butter and a little chopped parsley; heat all by setting the cup in boiling water; add the gravy from the dripping-pan, and let boil up once; place the fish in a hot dish, and pour over it the sauce. Or an egg sauce may be made with drawn butter; stir in the yelk of an egg quickly, and then a teaspoon of chopped parsley.

242. Baked White Fish or Shad—Thoroughly clean the fish; cut off the head, or not, as preferred; cut out the backbone from the head to within two inches of the tail, and stuff with the following: Soak stale bread in water, squeeze dry; cut in pieces a large onion, fry in butter, chop fine; add the bread, two ounces of butter, salt, pepper and a little parsley or sage; heat through, and when taken off the fire, add the yelks of two well beaten eggs; stuff the fish rather full, sew up with fine twine, and wrap with several coils of white tape. Rub the fish over slightly with butter; just cover the bottom of a baking-pan with hot water, and place the fish in it, standing back upward, and bent in the form of an S. Serve with the following dressing: Reduce the yelks of two hard boiled eggs to a smooth paste with two tablespoons good salad oil; stir in half a teaspoon English mustard, and add pepper and vinegar to taste.

243. Boiled White Fish—Cover in a fish-kettle or tie up in a cloth, and suspend in boiling water sufficient to cover it. Let it simmer, allowing from eight to ten minutes to the pound; remove the scum as it rises; when about half done, add a little vinegar or lemon juice; take out, drain, and dish carefully without breaking; pour over it drawn butter, and sprinkle with fine green parsley, or garnish with sprigs of parsley, and serve an egg sauce with it. Lake or Mackinac trout may also be cooked in same manner.

244. Broiled White Fish or Shad—Of the two fish the former is preferable, not only for its flavor, but on account of the great number of fine bones in the shad. Clean, and in case a white fish is used, split down the back; if a shad, split open in front, and also make a slit along the backbone, so it will lie flat to broil. Put the fish first inside down on the gridiron—well greased—and when nicely brown, turn carefully over so as not to break the skin. For this purpose use a pan-cake turner. It should take about twenty to twenty-five minutes to be done thoroughly over live coals.

245. Broiled Salt White Fish—Freshen over night in sufficient buttermilk or sweet milk (skimmed milk will answer) to cover, placing it flesh side down. Broil same as in preceding recipe, and serve with a gravy of hot cream, to which is added a half spoon of butter; salt to taste.

246. Fried Fish—Most of the smaller fish (generally termed pan-fish) are usually fried. Clean well, cut off the head, and, if quite large, cut out the backbone, and slice the body crosswise into five or six pieces. Dip in Indian meal or wheat flour, or in beaten egg, and roll in bread or fine cracker crumbs—trout and perch should not be dipped in meal; put into a thick bottomed iron frying-pan, the flesh side down, with hot lard or drippings (not in butter, as it discolors the fish, and also destroys some of its sweetness); fry slowly, turning when lightly browned. The following method may be deemed preferable: Dredge the pieces with flour; brush them over with beaten egg; roll in bread crumbs, and fry in hot lard or drippings sufficient to cover. If the fat is very hot, the fish will fry without absorbing it, and it will be palatably cooked. When browned on one side, turn it over in the fat and brown the other, draining when done. This is particularly a good way to fry slices of large fish. Serve with tomato sauce; garnish with slices of lemon.

247. Brook Trout—These delicate fish are always fried. Wash and drain in a colander, split nearly to the tail, flour them nicely, salt, and put in a frying-pan, hot but not burning. If you use lard instead of the fat of fried salt pork, which is preferable, throw in a little salt to prevent their sticking. Do not turn them until sufficiently browned for the table. They are to be fried crisp, or only browned, according to fancy. They are nice fried and served with slices of side salt pork, when both should be done crisp. Cook and serve brook trout with their heads.

248. Fried Smelts—Fry with the heads on, same as brook trout. See No. 247.

249. Pan Fish—Fried—Place them in the frying-pan with the heads all lying the same way, and the spaces between fill in with smaller fish. When done to turn, place a plate over the whole and drain off the fat; invert the pan and they will be left unbroken on the plate. Put back the fat again in the pan, and when quite hot slip in the fish carefully, and when that side is also done, drain on the plate as before, and slip them on a hot platter for the table. With care they will be unbroken, and with the heads on will make a fine appearing dish.

250. Stewed Fish—Cut any kind of large fresh-water fish in slices across, an inch and a half thick, and sprinkle with salt. Boil two sliced onions until done; pour off the water and season with pepper and salt; add two cups hot water and a little parsley, and in this simmer the fish until done. Serve quite hot.

251. Boiled Salt Mackerel—After freshening, wrap a cloth around and simmer for fifteen minutes. It will be about done as soon as the water slowly reaches boiling. Remove it carefully from the cloth to a platter, skin side up if it be unbroken. Place on it the slices of two hard boiled eggs, and pour around it, not covering, a drawn butter. Trim the platter with leaves of parsley or celery. Salt fish is much sooner boiled than fresh fish, while excessive boiling hardens it.

252. Broiled Salt Mackerel—This is more particularly a breakfast dish, and may be freshened over night, placing the fish in cold water, skin side up. Broil quickly, but do not burn, placing the skin side next the gridiron, and turning it. A wire broiler is the best to broil it on. When done, slip it off on a hot platter, without breaking, and serve with skin side up. Garnish with parsley or slices of lemon laid on the fish.

253. Fish Chowder—The best fish for chowder are haddock and sea or striped bass, although any kind of fresh fish may be used, those having large flakes being preferred. Cut in pieces over an inch thick and two inches square; place eight good sized slices of salt pork in the bottom of an iron pot and fry crisp; remove the pork, leaving the fat; put in the pot a layer of fish, a layer of split cracker, and some of the pork chopped fine, with black and red pepper and chopped onions; then another layer of fish, another of cracker, etc., etc., until the pot is full; cover with water and stew slowly until the fish is perfectly done; remove the fish from the pot to a dish in which it is to be served, and keep it hot; thicken the gravy with rolled cracker or flour; boil up once, and pour over the chowder.

254. Salmon Gratin—One coffeecup of cold boiled salmon, pulled into flakes with a fork; mix with this half a cup of cold drawn butter, pepper and salt; fill small cup-cake tins or sauce plates; cover with fine bread crumbs; place in the oven and brown.

255. Crumbed Haddock—Remove the skin and bones from cold boiled haddock, and boil with half a small onion; pick the fish into flakes, and mix with each pint of fish one teaspoon salt, half a teaspoon of pepper and a cup of dry bread crumbs; fill a buttered dish half full and pour in what remains of the drawn butter, or make a cup full; add the rest of the fish, sprinkle crumbs over the top, moisten with the water in which the bones were boiled, and bake about twenty minutes. It should be more moist than scalloped oysters.

256. Pickled Halibut—Take a good shaped piece of cold boiled halibut, stick half a dozen cloves in it, put it in a bowl and pour over it hot vinegar in which has been boiled a small bit of red pepper and a blade of mace; next day arrange around the edge of a dish some fresh crisp lettuce leaves; place the pickled fish in the center and pour over it what remains of the vinegar.

SHELL FISH.

Oysters—*Note*—This succulent bivalve forms an important, and, in many localities, an inexpensive article of food. The great variety of ways in which they may be quickly and excellently cooked, render them prime favorites with nearly every housewife. They are in their best season from September to April—the months spelled with an "r"—and were formerly considered quite unwholesome during the others. New methods of cultivation have, however, so far improved them, that they are now eaten in large cities, more or less, all the year round.

Oysters in the shell must be kept in a cool cellar, in conical-shaped heaps, occasionally sprinkled over with Indian meal or middlings, and drenched with salt water. In this way, and if free from frost, they may be kept sound for considerable time. Opened oysters, or oyster meats, come both canned, and in bulk by measure. They were formerly put up in kegs, but this method has been entirely superseded by the cans. In some localities the largest of selected oysters are termed "Counts," and are sold by the hundred, and not by measure or canned: They are larger and whiter, but not of so fine flavor as the smaller or less cultivated varieties, the small, uncultivated native, when fresh, being the sweetest of all. Of the canned oysters, the larger are termed "Selects," X X X, "Stars," or other fanciful names given by different oyster packers. The smaller kinds are known as "Standards," one X, etc.

When shell oysters are fresh, the shell is firmly closed; if partly open and it does not immediately close upon being touched, the oyster is dead and unfit for use. When canned oysters are spoiled or sour, the cans will be swelled on the sides; never buy such. Freezing is quite injurious to oysters, as it kills them in the shell, and destroys, in a great measure, the flavor of those in cans. Do not let oysters cooked in any manner stand, but serve them at once, as one great merit lies in their being eaten hot.

257. Roast Oysters in the Shell—Select the large ones, those usually termed "Saddle Rocks," formerly known as a distinct variety, but which are now but the large oysters selected from any beds; wash and wipe them, and place with the upper or deep shell down, to catch the juice, over or on live coals. When they open their shells, remove the shallow one, being careful to save all the juice in the other; place them, shells and all, on a hot platter, and send to table hot, to be seasoned by each person with butter and pepper to taste. If the oysters are fine, and they are just cooked enough and served all hot, this is the paramount luxury in oyster eating.

258. A Fulton Market or Eighteen-Penny Roast—Is still known in New York from the place at which it was and is still served, and from the original price of the dish. Take nine large oysters, wash, dry and roast over a charcoal fire. Two minutes after the shells open, they will be done. Take them up quickly, saving the juice in a small, shallow tin pan; keep hot until all are done; butter, sprinkle with pepper, and serve quickly.

259. Oysters in the Shell—Open the shells, keeping the deepest ones for use; melt some butter, season with minced parsley and pepper; when slightly cooled, roll each oyster in it, using care that it drips but little, and lay it in a shell; add to each a little lemon juice, cover with bread crumbs, place in a baking pan, and bake in a quick oven. Just before they are done, add a little salt. Serve in the shells.

260. Raw Oysters—On Half Shell—The finest for eating raw are those known as Shrewsburys, Blue Points or Cherry Stones—the names of the beds from which they are taken. Wash the shells, open them, and detach the upper or deep shell; loosen from the under shell by cutting the muscle clear—some term it the heart; serve six or nine to a plate, with a quarter of a lemon—to squeeze over them—in the center. Serve finely shaved white cabbage with them.

261. Raw Oysters—Without the Shells—Carefully open shell oysters, drain well in a colander, sprinkle with plenty of pepper and a little salt, place on the ice or a cool place, until served with Chili or Worcestershire sauce, horse-radish, lemon, or vinegar; also cut cabbage or pickled gherkins.

262. Boiled Shell Oysters—Wash the shells very clean, put in a small wire basket, suspend in a kettle of boiling water, and when the shells open lift the basket, remove the upper shell, and serve on a hot platter unseasoned.

263. Broiled Oysters—On the Half Shell—Select large ones, clean the shells, and open, saving the juice; put the oysters in boiling water a few minutes; take out and place each in a deep shell, with some juice; place on a gridiron over a brisk fire, and when they begin to simmer season with butter, salt and pepper, and a drop of lemon juice if desired. Serve on the half shell, with celery as a relish.

264. Broiled Oysters—Select large Count oysters, or shells that are just opened, dry them in a napkin, and broil on a fine wire broiler, turning frequently to preserve the juice. Serve quickly in a hot dish, with small bits of butter over them.

265. Broiled Oysters—Dry a quart of oysters in a cloth, dip each in melted butter well peppered, and then in dry bread or cracker crumbs, also peppered; broil on a wire broiler over live coals five to seven minutes. Serve hot.

266. Grilled Oysters with Pork—On a small wire, bent in shape of a hairpin, string alternately, first a large oyster, then a small slice of salt pork, until the wire is full; fasten the ends into a long wooden handle, and hold before the fire until all are well browned. Serve with or without the pork, as preferred, seasoned with pepper.

267. Steamed Oysters—Shells—Put some shell oysters in an air-tight vessel, the upper shell downwards, to save the juice when they open; set them over a pot of boiling water, and boil it hard for twenty minutes, or steam until the shells open, when they are done. Serve in the shells immediately, to be seasoned with salt and butter as eaten.

268. Steamed Oysters—Wash and drain a quart of Counts, or Select oysters, put them in a pan and place in a steamer over boiling water; cover and steam till they are plump, with the edges ruffled and black. Place in a heated dish with butter, pepper and salt, and serve.

269. Panned Oysters—Cut some stale bread in thin slices, taking off all the crust; round the slices to fit patty pans; toast, butter, place them in the pans and moisten with three or four teaspoons of oyster liquor; place on the toast a layer of oysters, sprinkle with pepper and put a small piece of butter on top of each pan; place all the pans in a baking pan and place in the oven, covering tightly. They will cook in seven or eight minutes if the oven is hot; or, cook till the beards are ruffled; remove the cover, sprinkle lightly with salt, replace and cook one minute longer. Serve in the patty pans. They are delicious.

270. Panned Oysters—Lay in a thin pie tin or dripping pan half a pint of large oysters, or more if required; have the pan large enough so that each oyster will lie flat on the bottom; put in over them a little oyster liquor, but not enough to float; place them carefully in a hot oven and just heat them through thoroughly—do not bake them—which will be in three to five minutes, according to fire; take them up and place on toast, first moistened with the hot juice from the pan. Are a very good substitute for oysters roasted in the shell, the slow cooking bringing out the flavor.

271. Oyster Stew—Put the liquor from the oysters on the stove, let boil, skim and season with butter and pepper; add the oysters. Let it come to a boil only. Season with salt and serve.

272. Oyster Stew—Take twelve to fifteen good sized opened oysters—those opened fresh from the shells preferred; place in half pint cold water in a stew pan; heat gradually until hot, skimming off all scum as it arises; when quite hot add half a pint warm milk; season with butter, pepper and salt if it requires it. Let it boil up once only, and serve in bowls or soup plates. Celery and cold raw cabbage to be served with it.

273. Plain Oyster Stew—Same as a milk or cream stew (see No. 274), using oyster liquor or water instead of milk or cream, adding more butter after taking up.—*Boston Oyster House, cor. Madison and Clark streets, Chicago.*

274. Oysters Stewed in Milk or Cream—Take half a pint good milk or cream, bring it to a boil, place in it one dozen medium sized oysters, and cook three to four minutes on a stove or range; season while cooking. Is a dish for one only. Use a like quantity for each additional person, but use all milk, or half each of milk and cream.—*Boston Oyster House, cor. Madison and Clark streets, Chicago.*

275. Dry Oyster Stew—Take six to twelve large oysters and cook them in half a pint of their own liquor; season with butter and white pepper; cook for five minutes, stirring constantly. Serve in hot soup plates or bowls.—*Boston Oyster House, cor. Madison and Clark streets, Chicago.*

276. Boston Fancy—To six or eight count or shell oysters use a half cup water or oyster liquor, season well with butter and pepper, and cook from three to five minutes, stirring constantly; serve on pointed slices of buttered toast standing in a bowl or soup plate, the points outward.—*Boston Oyster House, cor. Madison and Clark streets, Chicago.*

277. Neptune Oyster Stew—Six or eight shell oysters and four clams, just from the shells; stew four or five minutes in clam and oyster liquor mixed; add boiling milk or cream, and serve. It is quite necessary to add the milk quite hot, to prevent being soured by the clam juice.—*Boston Oyster House, cor. Madison and Clark streets, Chicago.*

278. Fried Oysters—Pour the liquor from the oysters; dip them in an egg batter made of two eggs, well beaten, and milk to thin to about as thick as cream; after dipping, roll the oysters in cracker meal, and fry in hot lard until nicely browned on both sides.—*Boston Oyster House, cor. Madison and Clark streets, Chicago.*

279. "Our Boston Fry"—Prepare the oysters in egg batter and fine cracker meal; fry in butter over a slow fire for about ten minutes; cover the hollow of a hot platter with tomato sauce; place the oysters in it, but not covering, garnished with chopped parsley sprinkled over the oysters.—*Boston Oyster House, cor. Madison and Clark streets, Chicago.*

280. Fried Oysters—For small oysters, drain them carefully; remove all bits of shell; sprinkle with pepper and salt, and set in a cool place ten to fifteen minutes; then, if oysters are quite small, pour them into a pan of fine rolled crackers, add the liquor, mix well, and let stand five minutes; add a very little salt and pepper, and mould into small cakes, with two or three oysters in each; roll into more dry cracker until well crusted, and fry in hot lard and butter, or beef drippings. Serve hot on a covered dish.

281. Fried Oysters—Dip them in the yelk of egg well beaten and seasoned, then in corn meal with a little baking powder mixed with it, and fry in hot lard like doughnuts; when hot enough the lard will cease to bubble, and remain quite still; skim out quickly and drain; or, if you have a wire frying basket, place them on that and put it in hot lard. If the fat is not perfectly clear, drop in a small peeled potato before frying, which will not only have the effect of clearing the fat, but also prevent its becoming too hot while frying. It is better not to touch oysters with the hand while preparing them for frying, as it tends to toughen them. All the turning and dipping can be well performed by the aid of a silver four-tined fork.

282. Broiled Oysters—Prepare oysters the same as for frying; grease a fine meshed wire broiler with salt pork, and broil over an open charcoal or coke fire, until browned on both sides. Serve on toast, with a cream sauce, in which sprinkle a little chopped celery and parsley.—*Boston Oyster House, cor. Madison and Clark streets, Chicago.*

283. Fricasseed Oysters—Take a slice of raw ham, which has been pickled but not smoked, and soak in boiling water for half an hour; cut it in quite small pieces, and put in a saucepan with two-thirds of a pint of veal or chicken broth, well strained, the liquor from a quart of oysters, one small onion minced fine, and a little chopped parsley, sweet marjoram, and pepper; let them simmer for twenty minutes, and then boil rapidly two or three minutes; skim well, and add one scant tablespoon corn-starch mixed evenly in one-third cup of milk; stir constantly, and when it boils add the oysters and one ounce butter; after which just let it come to a boil, and remove the oysters to a deep dish; beat one egg, and add to it gradually some of the hot broth, and when cooked stir it into the pan; season with salt, and pour the whole over the oysters. When placed upon the table, squeeze the juice of a lemon over it.

284. Oyster Pies—For each pie take a tin plate half the size around of an ordinary dinner plate; grease it and cover the bottom with a puff paste, as for pies; lay on it five or six select oysters, or enough to cover the bottom; butter them and season with a little salt and plenty of pepper; spread over this an egg batter, and cover with a crust of the paste, making small openings in it with a fork. Bake in a hot oven fifteen to twenty minutes, or until the top is nicely browned.— *Boston Oyster House, cor. Madison and Clark streets, Chicago.*

285. Oyster Pie—Line a deep pie-dish with puff paste, dredge with flour, pour in a pint of oysters, season well with bits of butter, salt and pepper, and sprinkle flour over all; pour on some of the oyster liquor, and cover with a crust, having an opening in the center to allow the steam to escape.

286. Oyster Pie—Line the pie-dish half way up with a good pie crust, fill the dish with pieces of stale bread, cover with a paste, and bake about twenty minutes in a brisk oven; take off the crust, have ready some nicely stewed oysters, or prepared as if for patties, fill the pie with them, replace the crust, and serve at once.

287. Oyster Pie—Line a dish with a good puff paste, putting an extra layer around the edge, and bake in a brisk oven; after baking, fill with oysters, season with pepper, salt, and one tablespoon of butter; sprinkle lightly with flour, and cover with a thin crust of the paste; bake quickly. When the top crust is done the pie will be ready to take out. Serve promptly, as the crust quickly absorbs the gravy. Some like this cold for picnics or traveling.

288. Escalloped Oysters—Cover the bottom of a well-buttered baking dish with a layer of bread or cracker crumbs, and wet them with half cup of cream or milk, put on in spoonsful; salt and pepper, and add bits of butter; then add one quart oysters, with the liquor; pepper and drop on small bits of butter; over these sprinkle thickly a layer of crumbs, wet them, and put on more butter; cover over tightly, and bake from half to three-quarters of an hour, or until the juice bubbles up; remove the cover, and brown over the top in a hotter part of oven for a few minutes. Serve in the baking-dish.

289. Oysters with Veal—(See VEAL WITH OYSTERS, No. 172.)

290. Oyster Fritters—Select plump, good-sized oysters; drain off the juice, and to a cupful of which add a cup of milk, two or three eggs, salt and pepper, and flour enough to make a rather thick batter; take up an oyster, cover it well with the batter, and drop in hot lard to fry, same as other fritters.

291. Oyster Croquettes—(See CHICKEN AND OYSTER CROQUETTES, No. 193.)

292. Oyster Patties—Put fifty freshly opened oysters into a sauce pan over a quick fire; let them boil, and skim; strain them quite dry saving the liquor; take of butter and flour each a tablespoon and a half; mix well together; let simmer over the fire until clear; then add the oyster liquor and a pint of cream; season with salt, pepper and a little nutmeg, and a very little cayenne; let all boil about twenty minutes, strain, add the oysters and finish with a little butter. The patties should be ready; place a spoonful of the stew in each; put on the cover and serve.—*Fermand Féré, Chef de Cuisine, Astor House, N. Y.*

293. Oyster Patties—(See VEAL PATTIES, No. 175). Stewing the oysters in the ordinary way, without pork or celery seasoning.

294. Deviled Oysters—Wipe them dry, and lay in a flat dish; cover with a mixture of melted butter, cayenne pepper—or pepper sauce—and lemon juice; let them lie for ten minutes, turning frequently; roll in cracker crumbs, then in beaten egg, and again in the crumbs; fry in hot lard and butter, mixed half and half. Serve quite hot.

CLAMS.

Note.—There are several varieties of clams, the round or hard-shell (known on the sea coast as quahogs) being in most common use, are the coarser kind, and quite strong in flavor. The more delicate kinds are little-necks, princes-bays, and soft-shells (the latter being in season during the cold months only, and should especially be fresh). Without possessing the delicate flavor of the oyster, they may be readily prepared in many ways to form a very desirable edible, while some of the dishes given are held in great estimation, particularly at the seaside.

295. Clam Chowder—(*The New Bedford Recipe*)—The materials needed are fifty round clams (quahogs), a large bowl of salt pork cut up fine, the same of onions finely chopped, and same (or more if you desire) of potatoes cut into eighths or sixteenths of original size; wash the clams very thoroughly, and put them in a pot with half a pint of water; when the shells are open they are done; then take them from the shells and chop fine, saving all the clam water for the chowder; fry out the pork very gently, and when the scraps are a good brown, take them out and put in the chopped onions to fry; they should be fried in a frying-pan and the chowder-kettle be made very clean before they are put in it, or the chowder will burn. (The chief secret in chowder-making is to fry the onions so delicately that they will be missing in the chowder.)

Add a quart of hot water to the onions; put in the clams, clam-water and pork scraps. After it boils, add the potatoes, and when they are cooked, the chowder is finished. Just before it is taken up, thicken it with a cup of powdered crackers and add a quart of fresh milk. If too rich, add more water. No seasoning is needed but good black pepper.

296. Clam Chowder—Take fifty quahogs and chop them up; peel and slice ten raw potatoes; cut into dice size six onions and half a pound fat salt pork; slice six tomatoes or use a large cup of canned tomatoes; one pound Boston or pilot crackers (sea biscuits). First put the pork in the bottom of the pot and try out; partly cook the onions in pork fat and remove; lay in the pot alternately the different ingredients as prepared, season with pepper and salt, cover with water and boil an hour and a half, with an inverted plate over to keep in the steam. Stir in a little chopped parsley just before taking up, as it will add to the appearance if not flavor of the dish.

297. Clam Stew—Take half a peck hard-shell clams, wash them clean, and put them in a kettle with about one cup water; let them steam until they open; take them out and remove from the shell, saving the juice; strain it, and with the clams return to the pot; after coming to a boil, add a pint milk, an egg-sized lump of butter, three crackers rolled fine, pepper, and salt if needed, which it will probably not.

298. Clam and Oyster Stew—Use about half the quantity of clams and proceed as above, using the same quantity of canned or count oysters as that of clams after they are taken from the shells, and cook as above directed.

299. Fried Clams—Take a sufficient quantity of shelled clams, and after drying, fry in a very little lard or butter, turning them over once or twice; just before they are done prick them with a fork to let out the juice, and add a little vinegar; when it is hot take up and serve.

300. Fried Clams—Breaded—Take from the shell some good sized soft-shell clams; beat an egg well, and add to it two tablespoons water, dry the clams well in a cloth, and dip them first in egg and then in fine crackers or bread-crumbs, and fry in good sweet lard or butter. They should fry considerably longer than oysters prepared in a similar manner.

301. Clam Pie—Of either hard or soft shell clam meats, take about three pints—if large, chop them up a little—having saved all their juice when opening, boil them in it; if not sufficient, add a little water; have at hand four medium sized boiled potatoes cut into small squares; make a nice pie crust, with which line a good sized earthen baking dish for half way down the sides. Place a small teacup in the middle of the dish, inverted to hold up the crust, and place around it first a layer of clams, and then a few squares of potato; season with bits of butter and a little salt or pepper, and dredge over with flour; repeat this until the dish is full, adding clam juice and a little water if necessary.

302. Clam Fritters—Put into an earthen dish three spoons of flour, a teaspoon of yeast powder, and two eggs; mix this with a little clam juice; mince a pint of clams and mix with this batter; put two or three spoons lard into a shallow frying-pan, and when hot, put in the clam batter by spoonfuls to fry; turn them over after three or four minutes, let them fry a moment longer, then take them out, and after draining them on a cloth, serve. Clam fritters should not be cooked in large masses.—*Emil Combe, Chef de Cuisine, Hotel Wellington.*

303. Clam Fritters—Take raw clams fresh from the shells and chopped fine; make a batter of the juice, an equal quantity of sweet milk and four eggs to each pint of the liquid, with sufficient flour to stiffen; fry in boiling lard the same as other fritters.

LOBSTERS, CRABS, ETC.

Note—Lobsters are seasonable all the year, but best from March to October. The flesh of the male lobster is the firmer, but the female is valued for its coral, lying inside the tail, which is used in several sauces and decorations on account of its beautiful color. Contrary to much prejudice on the subject, all parts of the lobster are wholesome except the stomach lying just back of the head and a black or bluish vein running from near the head to the extremity of the tail. These should be removed after it is boiled. The liver, frequently rejected from its being a greenish color when boiled, is, in fact, the most delicate part of the fish. Always buy a lively lobster—never a dead one—and boil it yourself, as they should be alive when put into the pot. Dead lobsters will be watery, soft, and not full when boiled. The smaller lobsters are the best—those weighing from one and a half to three pounds—and should be weighty as compared to bulk. Should ready-boiled lobsters be purchased, test them by gently drawing back the tail part way, which should rebound with a spring if it was not dead before boiling, in which case it should be rejected.

304. Boiled Lobster—The lobster suffers less upon being killed in cold water made hot, as it is dead as soon as it becomes warm, and the flesh will also be firmer. It requires from fifteen to thirty minutes to boil, according to size; qui.e large ones perhaps an hour. When boiled take it from the kettle, split it in half from the head to tail, remove the stomach and vein, crack the claws so that the meat may be removed readily, and serve on a platter. Lettuce and other concomitants of a salad should also be placed on the table or platter.— *Peirre Blot, Prof. of Gastronomy, Etc.*

305. Steamed Lobsters—Many persons think the lobster quite superior when steamed instead of boiled—the meat is dryer and finer. Place them in a steamer or fish-kettle, the boiling water not touching the fish, and steam twenty to thirty minutes, or until it turns a bright red color; take out, and dress in any manner as though boiled.

306. Lobster Croquettes—Take any of the lobster remaining from table, and pound it until the dark, light meat and coral are well mixed; put with it not quite as much fine bread-crumbs; season with pepper, salt and a very little cayenne pepper; add a little melted butter, about two tablespoons, if the bread is rather dry; form into egg-shaped or round balls; roll them in egg, then in fine crumbs, and fry in boiling lard.

307. Deviled Lobsters—Take out all the meat from a boiled lobster, reserving the coral; season highly with mustard, cayenne, salt and some kind of table sauce; stew until well mixed, and put it in a covered saucepan, with just enough hot water to keep from burning; rub the coral smooth until it is thin enough to pour easily, then stir it into the saucepan. The dressing should be prepared before the meat is put on the fire, and which ought to boil but once before the coral is put in, stir in a heaping tablespoon of butter, and when it boils again it is done and should be taken up at once, as too much cooking toughens the meat.

308. Scalloped Lobster—Butter a deep dish, and cover the bottom with fine bread-crumbs; put on this a layer of chopped lobster, with pepper and salt; so on alternately until the dish is filled, having crumbs on top. Put on bits of butter, moisten with milk, and bake about twenty minutes.

309. Crabs—Are boiled like lobsters, and may be served the same as lobsters in a salad. When well washed and cleaned put them in a sauce-pan, with slices of onion, carrots, parsley, chives if you have them, thyme, bay leaves, salt and pepper corns; half cover them with white wine, add butter, and put over a good fire to boil till done.

310. Soft Shell Crabs, Fried—Prepare the crabs by cutting off about one-fourth of an inch of the front part or mouth, and scraping out the fins from both sides under the shell, after which rinse well in cold water; fry in butter or good lard until a little crisp; when nearly cooked the shell turns red. Some prefer them breaded the same as oysters. Serve on toast with a butter sauce. Garnish with a few sprigs of parsley and some slices of onion, either or both.—*Boston Oyster House, cor. Madison and Clark Sts., Chicago.*

311. Boiled Hard Shell Crabs, Long Island Style—Use a deep pot and fill it half full of seaweed or twigs; put in enough sea water or salted water to cover the seagrass or twigs and bring it to a boil; then fill the pot with the crabs, which have been previously pricked with a fork to let the water out, cover, and keep the water boiling until the crabs are of the proper redness. This gives you your crabs free from water.

312. Deviled Crabs—Prepare same as deviled lobster, substituting for the coral and vinegar some fine cracker, first moistened with a tablespoon of cream. It may be served in the back shell of the crab. Serve with cream, crackers, and put a sprig of parsley on each shell, ranging them on a large platter.

313. Shrimps—Boil and shell them; serve hot with tomato, Chili or any other desired sauce or catsup.—*Boston Oyster House, cor. Madison and Clark Sts., Chicago.*

314. Terrapin in Chafing Dish, Maryland Style—First cut their heads off, then place them in a pot of boiling water; let them boil until the shell begins to peel; then take off the shell (which will come off very easily if boiled enough), remove the gall, sand bag and entrails; the balance is good; place in a chafing dish with spirit lamp under it (on your dinner table); season with red pepper, salt, and butter, one-fourth to one-half pound; add a glass of Madeira, let simmer for half an hour, but it must be stirred all the time.—*By an Old Member of the Maryland Club.*

FROGS.

Note—The French were the first among European nations to use frogs as food. Frog eating has become quite general in America, and they are now ranked as delicacies. Only the hind legs and quarters are used.

315. Frogs, Fried—The most popular way of cooking is frying, either plain, breaded or with an egg batter, the same as oysters, but longer, as they should never be underdone. They may be cooked in other ways as well.

316. Frogs, Stewed—Skin, boil five minutes, and throw in cold water to cool, and drain. Put in a stew-pan (for two dozen frogs) two ounces of butter; when melted lay in the frogs and fry about two minutes, tossing them in the pan occasionally. Put over them a teaspoon flour by sprinkling, and stir; add two sprigs parsley, one of thyme, a bay-leaf, ten cloves, a clove of garlic, salt, white pepper and half a pint of white wine; boil gently until done, and remove the legs; reduce the sauce by boiling, strain, and mix in the yelks of two eggs; pour over the legs and serve.

H. M. WILMARTH.   Established 1859.   T. W. WILMARTH.

H. M. WILMARTH & BRO.

Wholesale and Retail Dealers in

ARTISTIC GAS FIXTURES

225 and 227 State Street,

CHICAGO.

Western Depot for **MITCHELL VANCE & CO.**, Manufacturers.
Gas Fitting in all its Branches.

In addition to GAS FIXTURES we keep an assortment of the best Lamps for burning Oil. We have

The Cleveland Student Lamp,

The Manhattan Mammoth Student Lamp,

The best Library and Hall Lamps.

We keep the best BURNER ever invented for burning Oil, viz.

THE IMPERIAL BURNER

GIVING A LIGHT EQUAL TO 40 CANDLES.

We keep Rich Table Lamps made of Hammered Metal and other rare Materials. We also keep

Brass Fenders, Fire Sets, Andirons, Gas Logs and Sconces.

Send your orders for GAS FITTING to us and the work will be done promptly and at LOW PRICES and satisfaction guaranteed. We are the Agents for the celebrated GAS STOVE, manufactured by the American Meter Co. If you have not tried COOL COOKING, call and examine; we put them up on approval. We aim to please our customers both in quality of work done or goods furnished, and in the prices charged.

VEGETABLES.

Note.—The fresher all green vegetables are, the more wholesome; when they are so they break or snap crisply, but should they bend without breaking, or have a wilted appearance, they are stale. Most vegetables, if wilted, but not too badly, may be considerably restored by sprinkling with cold water and placing them in a cool, dark place. After being thoroughly washed nearly all vegetables should be placed in cold water for some considerable time before cooking. Soft water is much better to use for cooking vegetables, if pure and clean; but if hard water is used, have it freshly drawn, and put in a little soda to soften. Nearly all vegetables should be thoroughly cooked, and are spoiled if either over or underdone; those young and tender require less time than those more matured. All green vegetables, with some exceptions, should be cooked in plenty of salted water, putting them in at its first boil, as the evaporation tends to harden it; the quantity of salt to use is a heaping tablespoon to each gallon of water. All vegetables are done as soon as tender, and should then be immediately taken up and drained on a colander. Onions should be soaked in salted warm water previous to cooking, to partly remove any strong odor they may possess. Peas, string beans, and green corn should not be prepared for cooking until about ready to be used. Turnips, carrots, and onions should not be split, but sliced in rings across, as they thus cook sooner.

A little sugar added to turnips, beets, peas, corn, squash and pumpkin will improve them, particularly if poor. A very small bit of red pepper put in the water in which either meat or vegetables are boiled will, to some extent, deodorize the steam, and save the disagreeable odor arising from greens, cabbage, onions, green beans, mutton, corned beef, hams, etc., or a small piece of charcoal will effect the same object. When vegetables are to be served with salted meats, the meat should be cooked first, the liquor saved, and the vegetables boiled in it. Nearly all vegetables are injured by being boiled with fresh meat, and they also impart a bad flavor to the meat.

If home-grown, gather spinach, string beans, peas, asparagus, etc., early in the morning, when the dew is on, and put into cold water, until ready to be prepared for cooking—some add a little salt to the water—but if quite fresh, only let them remain in ten to fifteen minutes, and then drain. If purchased at market, and of doubtful freshness, let them lie longer in the salted water.

For general directions concerning potatoes, tomatoes, etc., see under each respective head. For celery, chiccory, cress, horseradish, lettuce, parsley, radishes, sorrel, for relishes or garnishes, see SALADS AND DRESSINGS, page 85.

317. Asparagus—*Note*—Gather with the morning dew upon it; do not cut it off, but snap it, avoiding the hard or woody part of the stalk; tie in bunches, eight to twelve stalks to the bunch, according to

size; when purchased the bunches come in much larger sizes, and should
be divided. If to be kept for some time before using (never more than
a day), place the bunch upright in about half an inch of cold water,
and keep cool. The larger stalks, or first cut, is prepared *vinegrette*,
with white sauce, or fried; the small ones, or second cut, like green
peas, and is better if taken from the water when still firm; if boiled
soft it loses its flavor.

318. Asparagus—Wash clean, break off the white part, and
put the green part into boiling water, slightly salted; boil five minutes,
and pour off the water; add more, boiling hot, and boil ten to fifteen
minutes; then put in a lump of butter, salt and pepper (some stir in a
thickening made of one teaspoon flour mixed with cold water); toast
three thin slices bread, spread them with butter, put in a dish and turn
the asparagus over it. The last water must be boiled down until just
enough for the gravy.

319. Asparagus—Make a gravy similar to the above, using the
water in which the asparagus has been boiled; cut the asparagus into
small bits, rejecting the white ends, and put it in a hot dish; turn the
gravy over it and serve.

320. Beans—*Note*—All stringed beans, as well as all green shelled
beans should be young and tender to be nice. There being many
varieties, they are in season from the latter part of June to the middle
or end of September.

321. Butter or Wax Beans—Cut off the ends of the pods and
carefully remove the strings from both sides; cut each bean lengthwise
in two or three strips, and soak in cold water for half an hour; take a
quart of dressed beans, considerably more than cover them with boiling
water, and cook until quite tender, when they will sink to the bottom.
They are better if boiled slowly for three hours. Drain well in the
kettle and return to the fire; add a dressing of half a gill of cream, one
and a-half ounces butter, one even teaspoon salt, and half a teaspoon
of pepper.

322. String Beans—Use two quarts of beans; string, snap and
wash them; boil in water enough to more than float them for fifteen minutes; draw off, and put on again in about two quarts of boiling water;
boil an hour and a-half, or till tender, and just before taking up, season
with salt and pepper, and stir in half a tablespoon butter rubbed with
two tablespoons flour and half a pint of sweet cream.

**323. Green String Beans (Snap Beans), French Haricots,
Kidney Beans, Etc., with the Pods**—Remove the string or thread
on both sides by partly breaking one end of the pod and pulling lengthwise; repeat on opposite end; cut them in half-inch pieces, soak in cold
water and put into boiling water with a little salt. Boil them until
cooked tender; take them from the fire and drain.

324. Green Shelled Beans—Boil for half an hour in water
sufficient to cover, and add a dressing in the manner as for string beans,
No. 322.

325. Dry Beans—Lima, White or Colored—*Note*—Dry beans should be soaked in water for some time, from five or six up to twenty-four hours, if a year or two old; if doubtful as to age, it will do no harm to soak them the longer time, and drain. If white beans are used, the smaller sized ones are the best. Their nutriment, although over-rated, is great, and for making a very palatable and cheap soup are very valuable.

To Boil—Put the beans in a saucepan with cold water, and boil gently until tender; as the water evaporates, fill up with cold water. Never use any salt in boiling dry beans, as it prevents their cooking. When boiled tender, drain, and they are ready to be baked, or used as they are.

With Pickled Pork or Bacon—Boil a quart of beans as directed above; cut in dice half a pound of salt pork or bacon—about medium fat and lean—and put it in a sauce-pan over the fire; when half fried, add the beans, mix and stir for a minute, and place in a warm oven for about twenty minutes, stirring occasionally; when done, sprinkle on the top some chopped parsley, pepper and salt to taste, if not already sufficiently salt. Ham or fresh pork may be used instead of salt pork or bacon, if preferred.

326. Boston Baked Beans—Soak in fresh water over night a quart of small white beans; in the morning change the water and put them in a porcelain kettle, with water enough to cover, and parboil until the skins wrinkle; then pour off that water, mix the beans with salt, and put them in an earthen bean-pot (do not use a tin pan); take a piece of fat salt pork, score the top and place in the middle of the beans; in a cup mix a tablespoon molasses, a teaspoon dry mustard, a half teaspoon of baking soda, and pour over the beans; fill the pot with warm water, cover the top with the earthen lid, and bake in a slow oven all day, being careful not to let the water dry out, and thus dry the beans; keep replacing the water until about three o'clock, and then let them remain in the oven untouched until four. If desired for supper, place in the oven about half an hour before, but add no more water, and do not have the oven too hot, so as to parch or dry the beans, the object being to have them moist, but hot, when served.—*Palmer House, Chicago.*

Either of the Brown Breads, Nos. 11, 12 or 95, should be served with the above.

327. Baked Beans—(See YANKEE PORK AND BEANS, No. 160).

328. Beets—Cut off the leaves, and in washing use care not to break off the little fine roots, which would let out the juice, and the beets lose their deep red color. They should be boiled in plenty of water; for young ones two hours, if old four to five hours; test them with a fork to see when tender; take them out, drop into a pan of cold water, and slip off the skin with the hands; slice them crosswise, and place in a dish; add salt, pepper, butter, and if not very sweet a teaspoon of sugar; set them over hot water to heat and serve hot, with or without vinegar. Should any remain put them in a stone jar whole, cover with vinegar, keep in a cool place, and use as wanted, slicing them then. A root or two of horseradish put into the jar will prevent a white scum arising on the vinegar.

329. Beets—Roast them in hot ashes or in the oven, turning them in the pan carefully with a knife, and when tender, peel, slice and dress with salt, pepper, butter and vinegar.

330. Harvest Beets—Take young beets, and after boiling and skinning, mash them with boiled potatoes, and season with salt and a large lump of butter, but no milk; place them in a dish, make a hole in the center, in which put a large lump of butter; sprinkle over with pepper, and serve at once. Called harvest beets, as at that time beets are quite young and sweet, and this dish is generally served at that season.

331. Beets Stewed—Clean and wash well, but do not skin them; put in an earthen vessel a layer of rye straw, moisten it slightly and place the beets on it; cover and place the vessel in a slow oven for five or six hours, then cool, skin and cut them in thin slices; melt some butter in a stewpan, and sprinkle in a pinch of flour, a teaspoon of chopped parsley, salt and pepper and then the beets; simmer twenty minutes, add a few drops vinegar, and serve.

332. Broccoli—Cook same as cauliflower (see No. 340).

333. Cabbage—*Note.*—Solid, hard heads should always be selected; soft ones are nearly worthless for almost any culinary purpose; never buy a cabbage that has the least rot about it. A slaw cutter is a very useful implement in the preparation of all sliced or shreded cabbage, for cold or hot slaw, etc.

To Boil.—Take off the outer leaves, wash thoroughly, cut off the stalk and stump, and put into boiling water, with a little salt and a small piece of charcoal, which will to some extent dispel the effluvia when boiling; boil slowly until tender; take up and drain in a colander.

334. Heidelberg Cabbage—Divide in halves two small but solid heads of hard red cabbage; lay the split side down and slice downwards the whole cabbage in narrow strips or shreds; put into a sauce-pan a tablespoon of clean drippings or any clear fat, and when hot put in the cabbage, three tablespoons vinegar and one onion, in which three or four cloves have been buried; boil two hours and a half; if it becomes too dry and is in danger of burning add a very little water.

335. South Carolina Cabbage—Slice or chop an ordinary sized cabbage quite fine, and cover it in a sauce-pan with boiling water; boil fifteen minutes; drain well, and add the following dressing: Half teacup white-wine vinegar, two-thirds cup of sugar, salt, pepper, half a teaspoon mustard, and two teaspoons salad oil; boil, and when hot, add a cup of cream and one egg stirred together; mix quickly and thoroughly with the cabbage; cook a moment, and serve hot.

336. Stuffed Cabbage—Cut out the heart of a large fresh cabbage by gently spreading back the leaves, to do which without breaking pour over it boiling water; fill the vacancy with finely chopped and cooked veal or chicken and rolled into balls with the yelk of egg. Tie it firmly together with twine, or tie it in a cloth and boil in a covered kettle two hours. This is a very fine dish and quite economical in using up cold meats.

337. Carrots, to Clean and Prepare—Trim off all the small roots; wash and scrape them gently, the skin only; wash well; drain and cut them in slices a quarter inch in thickness, either across or lengthwise.

338. Carrots, to Boil—When prepared as above, put them in a sauce-pan with a little salt and enough water to more than cover; boil gently until tender, and drain; the time will depend upon how young and tender they are.

339. Carrots Stewed—Divide them lengthwise, and boil till tender—from one to two hours; have ready a sauce-pan with one or two tablespoons butter and a small cup of cream; slice the boiled carrots very thin, and put in the sauce-pan; add salt, pepper, and let them stew ten or fifteen minutes, stirring gently once or twice, and serve in a vegetable dish. Carrots may also be boiled with meat, like turnips or parsnips, but take longer to cook.

340. Cauliflower or Broccoli, to Boil—Choose those very white, close and compact; trim off all decayed leaves, and cut the stock off close to the head; open the flower a little in places and wash; place them, head down, in salt and water for two hours previous to dressing, which will draw out all insects; put into boiling water, with a heaping tablespoon of salt to each two quarts of water; boil briskly fifteen to twenty minutes over a good fire, keeping the sauce-pan uncovered, skimming the water several times. When boiled tender, take up, drain, and if large heads, place upright in a dish, and serve with plain melted butter, pouring a little on the flower; or a white sauce or drawn butter may be used with it.

341. Green Corn—*Note*—There are many varieties of corn cooked in the ear, of which those known as "evergreen" and sweet corn are perhaps the best; it should be freshly plucked, and not taken out of the husk until just before being required to cook. It is best when eaten from the cob, with butter and salt.

342. Boiled Corn—After well cleaning the ears, removing all silk, and cutting off the end of the cob close to the corn, put them in salted boiling water; boil for an hour; or it may be boiled in the husk; remove the husk, and serve quite hot. When thoroughly cooked is a very enjoyable dish.

343. Stewed Corn—Carefully cut the corn off the ear, so as not to cut into the cob, and to three pints corn add three tablespoons butter, pepper and salt, with enough water to just cover; place in a stewpan, cover, and cook slowly, from half to three quarters of an hour, often stirring it, and adding more water if necessary; a few minutes before it is done, add half a cup of sweet cream, thickened with a teaspoon of flour. Some stew tomatoes separately, and mix with the corn just before serving.

344. Corn Oysters—To one quart grated green corn (that called evergreen is the best) add three eggs and three or four grated crackers; beat well, and season with pepper and salt; have ready in a skillet, butter and lard, or beef drippings, in equal proportions, quite hot, but not scorching; drop in little cakes about the size of an oyster, using a teaspoon for the purpose; when brown, turn, and fry on the other side, watching constantly to prevent burning. If the fat is just the right heat, the oysters will be light, and have much the flavor of fried oysters. Serve hot, and keep the dish well covered. By beating the whites of eggs to a stiff froth, and adding just before frying, they will be still better.

345. Corn Fritters or Mock Oysters—Grate six ears of corn, and mix with one tablespoon flour, two eggs; salt and pepper to taste; drop spoonfuls in hot lard and fry like oysters.—*Palmer House, Chicago.*

346. Cucumbers—Raw—Select those of medium size and very fresh, which have not lain in the sun after gathering, and put them in cold water half an hour; an hour before they are required peel thin, and slice on a slaw cutter set close, or very thin with a knife, commencing at the thick or blow end, or they are likely to be bitter; let the slices drop into a pan of cold water, in which let them lie for ten minutes; pour off the water and replace once or twice; finally cover them with ice, and set away in the refrigerator until wanted to serve, when salt and pepper them and pour over good cider vinegar; some add salad oil also.

From being an indigestible, strong and even dangerous edible, by this process they become wholesome and very relishable. Sliced onions are also served with them, but they should be mild, the Bermuda onion being the best.

347. Cucumbers—Boiled and Fried—Peel them, split them lengthwise in four parts; take out the seeds, and cut into pieces about an inch long; put them in boiling water with a little salt, and boil until cooked done; put them on a towel to dry; put some butter in a frying-pan, and place it over a good fire; when hot put in it some chopped parsley, salt, pepper; two minutes after, put in the cucumbers, fry a few minutes, tossing them now and then and serve.

348. Egg Plant—*Note*—The purple variety of an oval shape is the best. It should be firm, but not ripe.

Peel and slice one or two of medium size; put in cold water a little salted; boil until tender; drain, mash fine, season with salt and pepper, and add a beaten egg and a tablespoon of flour. Fry in little cakes in butter, or butter and lard in equal parts.

349. Egg Plant—*Another Method*—Cut in slices; lay in cold, well salted water for an hour or more; roll in egg and cracker crumbs, and fry with a little butter. Parsnips and oyster plant may also be cooked in same manner, but the latter should be made into smaller cakes, to resemble oysters.

350. Greens—The following plants and portions of young vegetables make good greens: Young beets, beet tops, cowslips, chiccory, chevel, dandelion, dock, horseradish tops, young turnips and tops, young milk weed, and many others peculiar to different localities. The dandelion and dock are especially fine, producing marked effects as blood purifiers and in clearing the complexion.

They should always be cooked in salted water, to which should be added a little soda or a pinch of carbonate of ammonia, to preserve their green color. All greens should be very thoroughly washed in several waters, after removing the roots and any dried or dead stalks which may have been gathered. They should be either cooked in soft water or water freshly drawn, and put in at its first boiling.

The time required is indefinite, depending upon how young they may be, or the variety used; are done always as soon as tender, and should then be taken up, and very thoroughly drained by placing in a colander, and squeezing with a wooden spoon.

351. Mushrooms—Although the majority of mushrooms are edible as well as very delicious, they differ so little in appearance from those that are poisonous—being of the same family—that the safest plan is to purchase only those canned or bottled. They are largely imported from France and Germany, and this industry is attracting considerable attention in this country. There are two kinds used here, the small or button mushroom, varying in size from as large as the thumb joint to a little larger, and a much larger variety termed the "umbrella," from its shape. Those which grow spontaneously are in season in September and October. Those cultivated from mushroom spawn are grown in cellars, or very rich damp ground.

The cooking of mushrooms may be readily summed up in the directions to cook the same as oysters, stewed, fried, broiled, or as a soup. They are made into various condiments, sauces and catsups, also dried and powdered, their flavor being added to meat gravies, game or soup.

352. Okra—Grows in the shape of pods, and is of a gelatinous character, much used for soup, and is also pickled; it may be boiled as follows: Put the young and tender pods of long white okra in salted boiling water in granite, porcelain or a tin-lined sauce-pan—as contact with iron will discolor it; boil fifteen minutes; remove the stems, and serve with butter, pepper, salt and vinegar if preferred.

353. Onions—There are many varieties, of which the Spanish, imported from Bermuda, are the mildest and best; a similar kind are grown to some extent in New Jersey.

354. Boiled Onions—Wash and peel; boil ten minutes; pour off the water, and add more boiling hot; boil a second time, and drain; pour on more boiling water; add some salt, and boil an hour; then place in a colander, turn a saucer over them, and press firmly to drive off all the water; put them in a dish; add butter and pepper, and serve. Old onions require about two hours to boil.

355. Baked Onions—Use the large Spanish onion, as best for this purpose; wash them clean, but do not peel, and put into a saucepan, with slightly salted water; boil an hour, replacing the water with more boiling hot as it evaporates; turn off the water, and lay the onions on a cloth to dry them well; roll each one in a piece of buttered tissue paper, twisting it at the top to keep it on, and bake in a slow oven about an hour, or until tender all through; peel them; place in a deep dish, and brown slightly, basting well with butter, for fifteen minutes; season with salt and pepper, and pour over some melted butter over them.

356. Fried Onions—Slice, and boil ten minutes at a time in three waters (unless the Spanish onions are used); drain, and fry in butter or beef drippings, stirring often; season and serve hot.

357. Onions with Beefsteak—See Beefsteak and Onions, No. 102.

358. Oyster Plant—Salsify or Vegetable Oysters—Wash thoroughly, scrape with a knife, cut across in rather thin slices, stew in water enough to cover them until tender, putting in a piece of salt codfish for seasoning, which remove before serving; thicken with flour and butter rubbed together; toast slices of bread, put in a dish and pour over; the codfish imparts an oyster flavor. Or, after stewing until tender in clear water only, mash, season with pepper and salt, and serve.

359. Boiled Parsnips—Wash and scrape them, and remove any black specks or blemishes, and if quite large, quarter the thick part. Put them into boiling water, salted with one heaping tablespoon to half a gallon water; boil rapidly until tender, drain, and serve in a vegetable dish; is usually served with salt fish, boiled pork or beef.

360. Stewed Parsnips—Wash, scrape and slice half an inch thick, put in a frying-pan with half pint hot water and a tablespoon butter, season, cover closely, and stew until the water is all cooked out, stirring to prevent burning; they thould be a cream, light brown.

361. Fried Parsnips—Scrape and slice them lengthwise, about a quarter inch thick, and fry brown in a little butter or clear beef drippings; if previously boiled, they will fry sooner, or the remnants of those boiled for dinner may be used.

362. Green Peas—Do not shell them much in advance of the time required to cook; canned peas should be rinsed before using; wash lightly two quarts shelled peas, and put into enough water to cover; boil twenty minutes, season, and add more hot water to prevent burning, if needed; also two tablespoons butter smoothly rubbed into two of flour; stir well and boil five minutes longer; should the pods be quite clean and fresh, boil tnem first in the water, remove and put in the peas. The Germans prepare a very palatable dish of sweet young pods alone, by simply stirring in a little butter with some savory herbs.

363. Peas Stewed in Cream—Into a sauce-pan of boiling water put two or three pints of young green peas, and when nearly done and tender, drain in a colander dry; then melt two ounces butter in a clean stew-pan, thicken evenly with a little flour, and hold it over the fire, but do not let it brown; mix in a gill of cream, add half a teaspoon white sugar, bring to a boil, pour in the peas, and keep the pan moving for two minutes, until well heated, and serve hot.

364. Dry or Split Peas—May be prepared and served in the same manner in every particular as dry beans, with the exception that they require to be soaked a shorter time before cooking.

Potatoes—*Note*—This fine esculent of the tuber specie is indigenous to South America, where it still grows wild, but is known to and provides food to more than half the civilized globe. It was early domesticated in Virginia, about Sir Walter Raleigh's time, from Chili or Peru, and was first introduced into England, about 1586; but little attention was given to it, and it is now but little over one hundred years since its cultivation has been common even in Ireland, where it saves half its inhabitants from fasting all the year round. It is said to have been introduced there at the time of a famine, from which fact, as well as its forming the chief food of the people, it acquired the name of Irish potato, which is now commonly used in contra-distinction to the sweet or yam potato.

The potato differs more than other vegetables in size, color, or quality, from the manner of propagation or species; it matures of all sizes, even in its kind, and distinct varieties are either white, pink, reddish, or blueish. Those properly cultivated in sandy soil will possess much starch, and, as a consequence, will cook dry and mealy.

The green appearance frequently noted upon the skin of either new or old potatoes is produced by what is known as *solanine*, arising from exposure to the sun's rays, when the tuber is grown quite near the surface or partly out of the ground, and even by long exposure to the light after being gathered. This is developed both in the sprouts and skin, and is very unwholesome, if not poisonous, imparting an acrid taste to the mouth and dryness to the throat. It should be always cut off, or the potato entirely rejected.

To Select—As a general rule the smaller the eyes the better the potato. Choose those of medium size, and smooth as possible. By cutting a slice off the larger end it may be discovered if sound; if spotted or have a large hollow they are not, and therefore inferior. Of the variety to select from it depends greatly on the season; some sorts keep better than others; others decay and go out of market as the season advances, while out of the hundreds of distinct species cultivated even in this country, each family will have its favorite. It is a fact, however, that those of forty years ago are scarcely to be found now, while those that supplanted them are again superseded by later and more improved productions yearly. Potatoes should be kept in a dark but cool and dry cellar, to prevent vegetating.

To Prepare—Old potatoes should be peeled before boiling or stewing, and immediately dropped into cold water, to remain until required, in order to save them clear in color, as exposure to the air darkens them; wipe each one dry before cooking; for the same reason, when sliced, let the slices drop into a pan of cold water to lie.

Peel matured potatoes as thinly as possible, as the better part lies nearest the skin. Scrape new potatoes also thinly—when quite young and tender the skins may be very easily removed with a scrubbing-brush—then drop them in water to keep them white.

To Cook—Steaming is now generally regarded as far preferable to boiling potatoes; first, from being more easily accomplished, and next, they cook a little sooner, and if watched, frequently tested, and taken up as soon as done, will preserve more of the starch, *i. e.*, be more mealy and dry. The great point in steaming, boiling or baking the potato is to know when done, and act accordingly, or they will be watery, or "soggy," as it is homely, but expressively, termed. For this reason, too, it is essential that potatoes of a uniform size should be selected for each cooking, commencing with the largest, and continue each time until the supply is exhausted. Quite large potatoes, for steaming or boiling, should be cut into four parts, smaller ones into two, and remove the middle or core, if hollow or defective, also all worm holes or other blemishes. Very old potatoes may be vastly improved by soaking in water over night; if quite watery, a small piece of lime dropped into the water in which they are boiling will cause them to cook dryer than without. Some kinds of potatoes boil in pieces before fairly done; some salt added to the water will obviate this; they will, however (as well as any other vegetables when salted), be longer in cooking. Either Irish or sweet potatoes, when frozen, should not be thawed before putting in to bake. New potatoes are better baked than by any other process of cooking, and should be scrubbed and rinsed very clean, many persons regarding their delicate skins the more edible part. New potatoes should be boiled in two waters; put on two kettles of water at the same time, place them in a wire basket, which set into one, and, when about half done, change to the other; matured potatoes will be the better by this process. Medium sized new potatoes will cook—boiled or baked—in twenty to thirty minutes; matured or old ones in about double that time, and either, when peeled, some fifteen minutes sooner. Of the various ways in which potatoes may be cooked, or the numberless dishes of which they form the whole or in part, hundreds of pages could be written.

365. Potatoes a la Parisienne—Wash and rub, with a coarse cloth or scrubbing-brush, new potatoes, drop into boiling water and boil briskly until done, and no more; press a potato against the side of the kettle with a fork; if done, it will yield to a gentle pressure; in a sauce-pan have ready some butter and cream, hot, but not boiling, a little green parsley, pepper and salt; drain the potatoes, add the mixture, put over hot water for a minute or two, and serve.

366. Potatoes a la Francaise (*French Fried*)—Peel and slice the potatoes as nearly the same size as possible; in a frying-pan have some hot butter or drippings, in which fry the potatoes until nearly cooked both sides; take them out of the fat and make it quite boiling hot; throw in the potatoes again for a minute or two until sufficiently crisp and they are done; putting them in a second time to the fat causes the slices to swell or puff up, which produces a light and desirable appearance and are delicious; after they are done place them in a cloth before the fire to drain out the grease; after sprinkling with salt, serve hot.

367. Lyonnaise Potatoes—One quart cold boiled potatoes cut into dice, three tablespoons butter, one of chopped onions and one of chopped parsley, pepper and salt; season the potatoes with the salt and pepper, fry the onions in the butter, and when they are yellow add the potatoes; stir with a fork, being careful not to break them; when hot add the parsley, and cook two minutes longer; serve at once on a hot dish.

368. Potatoes—Kentucky Style—Slice potatoes thin on a slaw cutter placed over a pan of water, and let stand half an hour, which hardens them; put them in a pudding-dish or dripping-pan, with salt, pepper and about half a pint of milk; bake for an hour, take out and add a lump of butter half the size of an egg cut in small bits and scattered over the top. The quantity of milk cannot be exactly given; enough to moisten the potatoes, with a little left as a gravy.

369. Saratoga Chips—Thinly peel and slice on a slaw cutter over a pan of cold water four large potatoes, using new when in season; salt the water and let stand while breakfast is preparing; take handfuls of the potatoes at a time, drain and dry them on a napkin; separate the slices and drop a handful at a time in boiling lard, without contact with each other; stir with a fork until a light brown or crisp, as desired; skim out, drain well and serve in an open dish. Are very good cold as well.

370. Tremont Potatoes—Take cold boiled potatoes of uniform medium size and split lengthwise into quarters or sixths; fry like doughnuts in boiling lard until the outside is browned or crisped; skim out and drain; before serving, sprinkle a little salt over them.

371. Ringed Potatoes—Peel some large sized potatoes, then cut them round and round as an apple is pared; fry in clean sweet lard like fritters until brown, drain on a sieve, sprinkle fine salt over them and serve.

372. Fried Raw Potatoes.—Pare and slice thinly into cold water some medium-sized potatoes, drain in a colander and put into a frying-pan in which is two tablespoons melted butter or clarified drippings, or half of each; cover closely ten minutes, removing only to stir them from the bottom to keep from burning; cook another ten minutes, stirring until lightly browned.

Sweet potatoes may be prepared in the same way.

373. Boiled Fried Potatoes.—After boiling let them cool, or use cold boiled potatoes; slice evenly, but only medium thin, and cook same as preceding receipt. They will cook in about half the time of raw potatoes.

374. Mashed Potatoes—*Note*—Simple as the operation would appear, some skill is required to mash potatoes properly, and for this purpose the old wooden masher is preferable to the perforated iron one more recently in vogue. When mashed they should be dipped out lightly into a hot covered dish and delicately shaped into a mealy heap, instead of being stirred, packed and patted into a rounded mass.

Pare potatoes and boil; drain and mash in the kettle until devoid of lumps; add milk or cream, butter and salt; beat like cake with a large spoon; the longer the better; turn them into a covered dish, smooth over the top, place a lump of butter in the center; do not serve them too moist.

Or, when mashed, add one or two eggs, well beaten; pepper and salt; put them in a baking dish, brush over the top with sweet milk, and place in a hot oven about twenty minutes.

375. Potato Balls—Mash six boiled potatoes and add enough cream or milk to make them a little soft; half a cup of grated ham—the bits too dry for other purposes may be grated—a teaspoon chopped parsley, and half a teaspoon each of pepper and salt, less of the latter if the ham is rather salt; mix all well and stir in the yelks of two eggs; form into little balls and fry a light brown. Serve with a good brown gravy.

376. Potato Snow—Take large and very white potatoes, free from spots or blemishes as possible, and boil them in their skins in salt and water until perfectly tender, but not overdone; drain and dry them thoroughly near the fire, and peel; put a hot dish before the fire, and rub the potatoes through a coarse sieve on to it; do not touch them afterwards or the flakes will fall; serve as hot as possible. Six potatoes is sufficient for three persons.

377. Potatoes for Each Day of the Week—On Sunday, peel, steam and mash; add milk, butter and salt, and then steam and beat up like cake batter until nice and light; the longer the better.—Monday, baked potatoes in the skins; be sure to take up when done, or they will be wrinkled and watery; if not served immediately, do them up in a napkin and tie close to keep hot.—Tuesday, peel them and bake with roast beef, cooking them under the meat.—Wednesday, prepare in Kentucky style (see No. 368).—Thursday, peel, steam and serve whole. —Friday, peel, cut in thin slices lengthwise, sprinkle with pepper and salt, and fry on a griddle greased with butter or beef drippings, and turn like pancakes.—Saturday, potatoes boiled in their jackets.

378. Sweet Potatoes—*Note*—There are doubts as to their origin, the evidence being in favor of both American and East India maternity; was known to Europe very long before the Irish potato. A variety known at the South as yam potatoes is regarded as one of the best, and are there generally called yams only. It is but a few years since they have been cultivated north of Virginia, but they are now produced in Ohio, Illinois and some other Western States and in New Jersey. Those from the warmer climates are yellow in external appearance, while those of the North vary from a dirty to a pinkish red. The best are brought from Carolina, Virginia or Georgia, and the next from New Jersey.

To Cook—The cookery of the sweet potato, yam potato or yam, may be briefly summed up by directions to cook them in all ways and particulars as directed for the common or Irish potato. They require a longer time to cook, however.

379. Sweet Potatoes—Dress them clean and bake in an oven an hour, or place in a steamer and steam from a half to three-quarters of an hour; or, when steamed and nearly done, scrape and peel them, place in a pan and bake half an hour; or, cut them (steamed or boiled) in slices and fry in butter or lard; or, peel and slice when raw, and fry a layer at a time on a griddle or in a frying-pan, with a little melted lard, using care not to cook them too long, or they will become hard; or, drop in boiling lard in a frying-pan, turn them till a nice brown on both sides; or, halve or quarter them and bake in a pan with roast beef, basting them often with its drippings.

380. Baked Sweet Potatoes—Wash, scrape and split them lengthwise; steam them half an hour, and then put them in a pan with lumps of butter, pepper and salt; sprinkle thickly with sugar, and bake a nice brown. Cook the Hubbard squash in the same manner, and with the addition of a little sugar they closely resemble this dish.

381. Salsify—See Oyster Plant, No. 358.

382. Summer Squash or Cymlings—By pressing the nail through the skin you can tell whether young, and consequently tender. If young, boil whole without peeling or removing the seeds, or cut across in thick slices; use as little water as possible (or steam them) for half to three-quarters of an hour; drain thoroughly; mash, and set back to dry out most of the remaining moisture for ten or fifteen minutes, stirring occasionally; then season with butter, salt, pepper and a little cream. If old ones are used, cut them up, take out the seeds, and season as above; they will require somewhat longer time to boil.

383. Winter Squash or Pumpkin—Cut them up, take out the inside; pare the pieces, and stew in as little water as possible; cook an hour; mash them in the kettle, and if too moist or watery, let it stand on the fire a short time until dry, stirring to prevent burning; season with butter, cream, salt and pepper. If not very sweet, a little sugar will improve it. They may also be steamed, and served either in the shell or scraped out; put in a pan mashed, seasoned as above, and again made hot before serving.

Hubbard squash may be baked in the same manner as sweet potatoes. See No. 380.

384. Tomato—*Note*—This highly popular vegetable, like the potato, is a native of South America. But little over fifty years ago the tomato was not used in the Northern States, and seldom in the South, and when grown it was as a curiosity or garden ornament.

The tomato is utilized in a great variety of ways, both when the fruit is green and ripe, being eaten raw, baked, boiled or stewed, while it forms an invaluable ingredient in soups, stews and sauces. It is made into condiments, as catsup or tomato butter, and pickled and preserved in various ways. The art of canning has also made it available all the year, in nearly as good a state essentially as the fresh fruit in season. It is thought to produce dietetic effects, and is doubtless one of the most healthful vegetables grown, either raw or cooked in any manner. In purchasing tomatoes, select those of medium size, solid and smooth skinned, and with the least warts or blemishes about the stem end.

385. To serve fresh Tomatoes—Pour boiling water on to the tomatoes until they are covered; cover and let them stand until the skins begin to crack, when they may be easily peeled; put them on ice, and let them remain until perfectly cold; then slice and serve with dressing, or with powdered sugar, salt, pepper, and vinegar. Claret instead of vinegar is considered by many quite a fine dressing, but use no salt or pepper. Never serve tomatoes without peeling.

386. Baked Tomatoes—Take eight or ten tomatoes, peel and slice rather thick, and put into a deep baking-dish; season liberally with salt, pepper, and two ounces butter; cover over with bread crumbs, and then pour over a little butter clarified by heating, and bake in a moderate oven a third to half an hour. Serve hot.

387. Stewed Tomatoes—After scalding and peeling, cut them into a stewpan; season and let them simmer (not boil) for three-quarters of an hour. May be cooked with soft bread-crumbs or small squares of bread, using nearly as much bread or crumbs as tomato, adding it after they are nearly done.

388. Stuffed and Baked Tomatoes—From the blossom end of a dozen tomatoes—smooth, ripe and solid—cut a thin slice, and with a small spoon scoop out the pulp without breaking the rind surrounding it; chop a small head of cabbage and a good-sized onion finely, and mix with them fine bread-crumbs and the pulp; season with pepper, salt, and sugar, and add a cup sweet cream; when all is well mixed, fill the tomato shells, replace the slices, and place the tomatoes in a buttered baking-dish, cut ends up, and put in the pan just enough water to keep from burning; drop a small lump of butter on each tomato, and bake half an hour or so, till well done; place another bit of butter on each, and serve in same dish.

389. Turnips—Wash, peel, cut in thin slices across the grain, and place in a kettle with as little water as possible; boil until tender and you can easily pierce them with a fork; drain well, season with salt, pepper and butter; mash fine and place on the stove, frequently stirring until all water is dried out; do not boil too long, as they are sweeter when quickly cooked. They may be steamed, instead of boiled, and in fact are finer in that way. They may also be baked.

390. Dried Turnips—Pare, slice and cut them in dice an inch square, boil till nearly done in as little water as possible, and to one quart turnip add a tablespoon of sugar, and salt to taste; when boiled as dry as possible without burning, add two or three spoons of cream, a beaten egg, and serve. Slices of turnip or parsnip left from a boiled dinner are nice browned in a little butter the next day.

Schenck's Adjustable

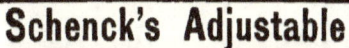

Any Housekeeper in the land can repair the Cook Stove—put in new Fire Backs, new Grates and new Linings—by using **SCHENCK'S ADJUSTABLE STOVE REPAIRS.** Sold by all Hardware and Stove Dealers. SEND FOR CIRCULARS. Manufactured only by

Schenck's Adjustable Fire Back Co.,
94 Market Street, CHICAGO.

IF TROUBLED by water beating under outside doors from storms, etc., send your address to HOWARD MFG. CO. 94 Market Street, CHICAGO.

A. HELLER. T. F. TALMAGE.

NATIONAL SPICE MILLS.

HELLER & TALMAGE,

Manufacturers and Dealers in

TEAS, COFFEES, SPICES

BAKING POWDER, EXTRACTS, ETC.,

No. 61 South Market Street, CHICAGO.

PRICE LIST FORWARDED ON APPLICATION.

We make a specialty in putting up our National Coffee in one pound package, far superior to any that is put up.

ASK YOUR GROCER FOR IT.

Phillip Best Brewing Company

OF

⤙MILWAUKEE, WIS.⤚

MANUFACTURERS OF THE CELEBRATED

Export,
Bohemian and Select
❖BEERS❖

AT THEIR

Empire & South Side Breweries.

CHICAGO BRANCH HOUSES:

Corner Indiana and Desplaines Streets,

Corner Halsted and Meagher Streets.

Bottling Department: Telephone 4383.

J. S. PIERCE, General Agent.

EGGS AND MACARONI.

Eggs—*Note*—The nutritive qualities of eggs are much greater than that of meat; those of different birds vary, however, in this respect. Those of the domestic hen are most esteemed and used; those of the turkey are nearly as mild as those of the hen, and that of the goose is larger, but about as preferable for most culinary purposes. Duck eggs have a richer flavor, but not so desirable to be eaten alone, although preferred by some, as either of the above. They are, however, as good for all purposes of cookery, and for puddings or custards are superior to any; when boiled they require less time than for those of the hen. The eggs of nearly all game birds are edible, and partake somewhat of the bird, and are generally colored or mottled. Those of the sea-fowl have a strong, fishy flavor and are little esteemed, while those of the plover, thrush, pheasant, etc., are highly so. The eggs of the turtle, consisting of yelk only, without shell, are very numerous, and are quite delicious.

The delicate nature of the egg render them acceptable to the weak stomachs of invalids, and they are quite nourishing when admissible, but will not agree with all. The yelk alone is the better for invalids, and will be frequently relished when the white would be rejected. Poaching is the lightest way of cooking eggs, and is simply a raw egg broken for a minute into hot water, being careful not to break the yelk. Eggs are also used in nutritive beverages, beaten up raw; the yelks alone are often used for this purpose.

To Select—Eggs are more wholesome soon after being laid, and the sooner they are used the better. There is probably nothing more vexatious to the housekeeper than for eggs to turn out addled in the act of using, for which reason care should be used in their selection. Do not rely upon the specious placard or assertion of tradesmen that their eggs are "*strictly fresh*," but examine each one yourself, and the result will repay the trouble. There are several methods to ascertain their state. First place the large end against the tongue; if slightly warm it is sound; or look through it before the sun or a light in a darkened room; if it looks clear and the yelk can be readily seen it is good, but if a dark spot appears it is the contrary. This last method is termed "candleing" by dealers; or they may be tested by placing in water sufficient to cover; those that lie flat are sound, but those that stand on end are unsound. When an egg emits a sound when shaken it is utterly decayed, and, of course, should be rejected. Eggs that are purchased and cannot be entirely relied upon should be broken separately into a cup; the stale egg will not then waste others. Eggs vary so much in size that they properly should be sold by weight; the average of full-sized, plump hen's eggs should be 22½ ounces per dozen, and those of the larger variety of hen's 24 ounces.

To Keep Eggs—Any method which will effectually exclude the air from the inside of the shell will preserve eggs for a certain time, and the following are among the best, some of the results of long experience by egg packers or dealers. Eggs for packing should not be more than one day laid, and packed in fine, clear weather, the best season being from April to September.

An old-time way of packing was to immerse them in lime water and set them away in a cool cellar; this, although usually successful for some weeks, often destroyed the eggs by keeping them in it too long, or the preservative was apt to be made too strong, and the shells were soon eaten; it also to some extent discolored the shell. A better manner and quite simple is to pack them in salt in a stone jar; a layer of salt two inches thick first, and alternate layers of eggs and salt to fill the jar, the eggs standing on the larger end, a thick layer of salt to cover the top; put on the stone cover and set in a cool, but not in a place where they may freeze in winter. Or put the eggs into a cabbage net or wire basket, twenty at a time, and hold them in boiling water for twenty seconds; no longer; repeat until all are boiled, and pack away in sawdust; they will keep for two or three months quite good enough for any culinary purposes. Or dissolve gum arabic (a cheap quality will do) to consistency of thin mucilage, and apply to each egg with a brush; pack them in powdered charcoal and place in a cool, dark place; wash when required for use.

391. Boiled Eggs—There is a very general mistake about boiling eggs. To be healthful and most digestible, the eggs should be cooked evenly, the white and yelk alike; in the rapid boiling by the usual rule of three to four minutes for soft, or five minutes for medium, the white becomes toughened before the yelk is scarcely cooked. To remedy this and render them not only more palatable and nutritious, and less indigestible, boil them in a vessel having a tight fitting cover (a common tin pail will answer admirably), put in the eggs and pour boiling water upon them, about two quarts of water to a dozen eggs; cover tight and set off the stove; in about seven minutes remove the cover, turn the eggs, replace the cover; in six or seven minutes more they will be done, if but two or three eggs; if more, in about ten minutes. Formerly, an egg boiler was a regular appurtenance of the breakfast table—an oval-shaped can six inches high, with capacity for a dozen eggs, which were placed on a movable rack like a castor, having large holes in which to set each egg; two lids hinged at either end closely covered it. Raw eggs were placed on the table with boiling water, and the duty of boiling them devolved upon the lady or daughter of the house. This is the nearest approach to the production of properly boiled eggs, as above given, and although long gone into disuse, it is one of the things to be regretted. It is, however, still in vogue in England—where it originated—in old families. By the ordinary methods, eggs boil soft in three minutes, medium in four, hard in five to six, and very hard, for garnishes or sandwiches, in ten to fifteen, provided the water is kept boiling from the time they are put in. They are less liable to crack when put in water not quite at the boiling point. Also place them in water carefully, one at a time, with a large spoon. Very fresh eggs require a little longer to cook, in any manner, than older ones.

392. Omelets—The variety of omelets made, especially by the French, who originated them, is very numerous. The filling, whatever it may be, is put in when it is folded or turned, and the manner of making a plain omelet will serve as to the material process for all. Among the fillings used are fine herbs (*Omelette aux Fine Herbs*), selecting any favored; any kind of preserves, jelly or jam (*Omelette aux Comfiture*), chopped boiled ham or bacon, cold veal minced; sweetened or flavored with vanilla, lemon extract or the yellow, not the inner rind (*Omelette Souffle*), minced onion, shallot or grated cheese; oysters are also used, by first scalding them in their liquor, removing the beards, and cut into small pieces. With the exception of the *Soufflé*, they are all made alike.

393. Plain Omelet—In compounding the omelet it is optional whether to beat the whole egg or to beat the whites and yelks separately, or to add flour and milk or milk alone; but if desired soft, milk should be used; when separated do not beat the yelk too much or they will be too thin; beat the white to a stiff froth and add lastly; melt about one ounce of butter for four or five eggs in a thin long-handled frying-pan very hot, next to burning; pour in the egg, which, if the pan is properly heated, will at once bubble up; break the bubbles, shake the pan continually, and slip a knife under frequently to prevent burning; and when the bottom is hard enough to hold together and the top partly cooked loosen up one side and turn it over the other, tipping up the pan at the same time on the side from which it is turned; the time to add any filling mentioned above is just before it is turned; place it on the egg in the cavity of the tipped pan and fold the other side over it; loosen the omelet free from the pan, and if desired browned on both sides, skillfully flap it over, let it brown a moment and slip it off the pan to a hot platter.

394. Plain Omelet—Having prepared the eggs as desired in quantity and ingredients, of egg, milk or flour, put about two ounces of butter in the pan (sufficient for eight eggs) and shake it about quickly to have it melt evenly, and cover the whole inside of the pan; as soon as very hot pour in the prepared egg, which stir and move about to cause it to cook as evenly as possible; should some part adhere to the pan raise it there with a knife, and adding a little butter, allow it to run under; it must be done quickly; when cooked soft or hard, to taste, run the knife under one-half the omelet nearest the handle, and turn that part over the other so as to nearly or quite double it; then, having an oval dish or small platter in the left hand, hold the pan with the right, the thumb lying along the handle instead of the fingers; incline the dish by raising the left side; place the front edge of the pan (opposite handle) on the edge of the dish, turn it upside down, and the omelet is dished, bottom or browned side up, and sightly.—*Prof. Blot.*

Three eggs make a good sized omelet for one or two; for more persons it is better to make several small ones than one very large one; omelets are generally preferred soft inside; they should be made quick, in three to five minutes.

395. Omelet Souffle—Separate the yelks from the whites of six eggs; add to the former five ounces powdered sugar and a tablespoon of flour (rice flour is best), and flavor with vanilla, orange flower water or lemon rind; stir all well together; whip the whites of the eggs and mix them lightly with the batter; put in a sauce-pan three ounces of butter, melt it over a bright but gentle fire, and when the omelet is set turn the edges over to make it of oval shape, and turn it off as directed above on to a granite or porcelain pie dish previously well buttered; place it in the oven and bake twelve to fifteen minutes; sprinkle finely powdered sugar over it and serve immediately; is sufficient for three or four persons.

396. Scrambled Eggs—Heat a cup of sweet milk, then rub a tablespoon of butter with a teaspoon of flour, and stir into the boiling milk. Into this put six well-beaten eggs and stir until thick.

397. Baked Eggs—Break eight eggs into a well buttered dish, put in pepper and salt, bits of butter and three tablespoons cream; set it in the oven, bake twenty minutes and serve hot.

MACARONI.

398. Macaroni—Originally only of Italian production, is now extensively manufactured and used in this country. It is produced from slightly-moistened wheat flour, pressed into hollow tubes by great force. The harder the wheat from which the flour is made the better. The best is of a yellowish color, swells to about four times its original bulk, and does not break in cooking.

399. Macaroni a la Riccadonna—Put a two-pound can of tomatoes in a sauce-pan and let simmer three to four hours, until they become quite thick and jelly-like; in the meantime take half a pound salt pork and one large onion, both cut into small pieces, and fry to a nice brown, taking care not to burn; pour them into the tomatoes, and let the whole simmer together; cover the macaroni with boiling water and boil for twenty-five minutes; drain, put on a platter, and pour over it the tomato sauce and put a generous sprinkling of grated cheese over the whole.

400. Macaroni—Boil the macaroni in water until tender, which will be about twenty minutes; mix a dessertspoon of flour with a tablespoon butter; add half a cup milk, half teaspoon mustard, the same of salt and pepper, a quarter teaspoon cayenne, and four ounces grated cheese; stir all together and boil ten minutes; drain the water from the macaroni and pour over it the dressing; boil up once and serve hot.

P. J. PROBECK,

No. 62½ N. Clark St.,

CHICAGO, ILL.

DEALER IN

CROCKERY, GLASS AND EARTHENWARE

Lamps, Cutlery, Etc.

FINE GOODS AT LOWEST PRICES

Housekeepers' Orders promptly filled and Goods delivered at any part of the city.

FULLER & MILLS,
(J. W. MILLS,)

SUCCESSORS TO

FULLER AND FULLER

(ESTABLISHED 1873.)

Steam Carpet Cleaning Works

70 & 72 W. Washington Street,

One block from carriage entrance to Tunnel.

THE BEST IS ALWAYS THE CHEAPEST!

If you want a Perfect Article, ask for

BELDING BROS. & CO'S

→❈SUPERIOR❈←

SPOOL SILKS

Sewing, Saddlers', Embroidery and Pure Thread Knitting Silks.

We manufacture the ONLY PURE THREAD KNITTING SILKS in the market, all others being made from Spun Silk, which has very little strength or durability, and is really not worth the knitting. Our Goods have taken the

First Premium Over All Competitors

at all places where placed on exhibition in contest for premiums. We have been awarded

Two Gold Medals,

the ONLY ONES ever awarded to any silk manufacturer in the world.

Our Goods are for sale by all prominent dealers in the United States, Canada, British Possessions, South America and Australia.

183, 185 & 187 FIFTH AVE., CHICAGO.

SOUPS AND BROTHS.

Soup—*Note*—To produce the most nutritious and palatable soups is an art in which the French especially excel, forming the greater part of the food of the people. Italian cooks also produce very fine pottage or broths.

401. Soup Stock—The foundation for all soups is lean meat—beef, veal or game—to which is added the broken bones of the same, of fowls, or small bits of ham bone saved from time to time, and boiled down in the *stock kettle*. When highly concentrated by boiling it will be a jelly-like compound, and the impurities having been precipitated it is left clear for ready use. For clear soups a white stock should be used, the base being veal or fowls, instead of beef. Soups are also compounded of different fish, shell-fish, frogs, etc., or of vegetables, of which dry beans or peas are prominent and very nutritious. The proportion of beef to use in compounding *stock* is a pound of meat to a quart of water. In using fresh meats for soups, instead of stock, put the meat, properly cut up, into cold water, and let it stand to draw out the juice until it begins to color the water, and then put in to boil. The soup is done when the meat is destitute of juice.

For either soup or stock the coarser parts of beef may be utilized, as the neck, flank or a soup bone (the shank of the fore-quarter or hock of the hind-quarter), the fat being mostly removed before boiling, and the balance can be entirely removed when cold. Mutton is too strong in flavor for good stock, and should not be used, while veal, although quite gelatinous, adds very little in nutriment.. Good soups are free from grease.

The seasoning or flavors for soups are quite numerous, and vary according to taste, the plainer having simply pepper and salt; the richer have many flavors, blended in such a manner that no one predominates; this is really the great secret in soup making. The herbs most in use by skilled cooks are sage, mint, thyme, tarragon, basel, parsley, bay leaves, sweet marjoram, summer savor; onions and garlic are used in such small quantities that they add their flavor almost imperceptibly. Of spices, cloves, mace, celery-seed, white, red and black pepper, or red capsicum pods in very small quantities. Macaroni, vermicelli, rice, sago, pearled barley (in mutton broth), generally afford, when used, their names to the soup, while vegetable soups are also compounded of onions, carrots, turnips, parsnips, celery, etc., all chopped and blended together, the proportions of each being *ad libitum*. Noodles also form a common addition to several soups. The best soup makers have a fine sense of taste, as the proportions of ingredients or flavors cannot be given by rule for the finer productions, but must be left to the judgment for delicacy in compounding.

When soups form the principal dish they should be richer than when they precede meats or fowls in regular course.

Thickened soups should be seasoned higher than thin ones, and white or clear soups should be strained through a hair sieve or fine cloth.

Coloring is used in some brown soups, the chief of which is burnt sugar; this it also known as caramel by French cooks.

The fat removed from soup or when compounding stock may be clarified by melting and pouring it in a bowl containing a little hot water. When cold, all sediment or impurities may be removed from the bottom of the jelly (or cake, if boiled down), and the clear fat utilized in many processes of cookery.

The more delicate flavors should be added to soups just before serving, or they will be destroyed by evaporation. Stock may be varied in flavor by the addition of a little anchovy or Worcestershire sauce, sugar, calve's foot or ham as predominant; vegetables boiled with stock will prevent its keeping. Bone and gristle, possessing the gelatine matter necessary to solidify, are requisite for stock to jell. Meat alone will produce a broth only equal to beef tea. Roast beef bones, or those of steak after cooking, make good stock by the addition of some fresh meat to furnish more nutriment.

402. English Game Soup (for 25 persons)—There are four stages in the production of this soup.

1. Make a rich broth of the bones and frames of two dozen, or more, prairie chicken or other wild birds; then put into a sauce-pan four large or six small carrots, two onions, a little celery and leek, two tablespoons salt, ten each of cloves, allspice, and pepper-corns, and a teaspoon of mace; add the broth, diluted with water to four gallons, if not that quantity; set all on a hot fire, and when it boils, skim; let it boil down to about a gallon and a half; then strain through a medium sieve, rubbing through it the vegetables and what meat comes off the bones; place it in another sauce-pan on the fire, and boil half an hour.

2. Boil the breasts only of six or eight prairie chicken, ducks, or other game birds, of dark meat (or venison may be used), in a portion of the broth; take them out, cut into squares or dice, and set aside, but kept warm until the soup is nearly completed.

3. Melt in a small stew-pan half a pound of butter, to which add two tablespoons browned flour and some of the broth; let it boil for fifteen minutes, and set aside to cool a little, when skim off all the fat; add a pint of sherry, half a pint of Madeira wine, and half a lemon, peeled and sliced; season with pepper and salt to taste; keep it hot.

4. Prepare some force meat balls in the following quantity for the above amount of soup: Half a pound of calf's liver chopped fine, two ounces beef suet or marrow, six ounces stale bread, grated and soaked slightly in sweet milk, and season with a little salt, pepper, nutmeg, sage, and ground cloves, well mixed; sift all, and add one egg and the yelk of another, together with sufficient flour to form a very thick paste, which put in a small tube formed of white paper, and drop out into hot water, bits about as large as a small marble; let them stand for ten minutes, and strain off. Lastly, put into the hot soup the diced breasts of game and the balls, and serve all hot.—*Constantine Wolf, Chef, Grand Pacific Hotel, Chicago.*

403. Mock Turtle Soup—Scald a well-cleaned calf's head, remove the brain, tie it up in a cloth, and boil an hour, or until the meat will easily slip from the bone; take out, save the broth, cut it in small, square pieces, and throw them into cold water; when cool, put it in a stew-pan, and cover with some of the broth; if not rich, add some stock jelly; let it boil until quite tender, and set aside.

In another stew-pan melt some butter, and in it put a quarter of a pound of lean ham, cut small, with fine herbs to taste; also parsley, onion shallots, and mushrooms (if in season, or canned ones may be used); add about a pint of the broth, let it simmer for two hours, and then dredge in a small quantity of flour; now add the remainder of the broth and a quarter bottle of Madeira or sherry, let all stew quietly for ten minutes, and rub it through a medium sieve; add the calf's head, season with a very little cayenne pepper, and perhaps a little salt, the juice of one lemon, and, if desired, a quarter teaspoon pounded mace and a dessertspoon sugar.

Having previously prepared force meat balls, No. 413, add them to the soup, and five minutes after serve hot.

Three or four pig's feet, well cleaned, may be used with the calf's head, should the quantity of soup required be considerable; at the same time the other ingredients should be increased proportionately.

404. Bean Soup—Very Cheap and Nutritious—Boil in two quarts water a small soup bone until the meat can be easily removed from the bone, which take out. Having soaked a cup of small white beans for two hours previously, put in and boil an hour and a-half, then add three potatoes, half a turnip, and a parsnip or carrot sliced fine or diced; boil half an hour more; just before serving, put in a handful of dry bread crumbs, and serve; if the flavor of onion or garlic is liked, add either, cut fine; of garlic the slightest quantity should only be used. A good soup may be had, for Saturday dinner, when preparing for Yankee Pork and Beans, No. 160, or Boston Baked Beans, No. 326, parboiling more beans than required to bake, and having taken out the necessary quantity, leave the remainder for the soup, and proceed as above.

405. Tomato Soup—One quart canned tomatoes, two heaping tablespoons flour, one of butter, one teaspoon salt, one of sugar, one pint hot water; let the tomatoes and water come to a boil; rub the flour, butter and a tablespoon tomatoes together, and stir into the boiling mixture; add seasoning; boil all together fifteen minutes, rub through a sieve and serve with toasted bread; this bread should first be cut in thin slices, buttered and cut into little dice, placed in a pan buttered side up and browned in a quick oven.

406. Tomato Soup—Peel and cut fine six good sized tomatoes and boil in one quart of water; after boiling a few minutes put in half a teaspoon of soda, one pint of milk; add butter, salt and pepper to taste. —*Palmer House, Chicago.*

407. Economical Soup, with Vegetables—Any piece of the coarse beef will do, or a soup bone is best; after washing well and cutting off most of the fat, put it in a kettle, with cold water enough for the soup; let it boil slowly from three to six hours, according to the quantity and quality. An hour before required, cut a solid head of cabbage in quarters, sprinkle it with salt, and put in the kettle, and a quarter of an hour after add a few turnips, whole potatoes if small, or cut in two if large; the two last should have been previously peeled and put in cold water for half an hour before; when all are done, remove the vegetables and meat to a steamer, to keep hot; should the quantity of soup be insufficient, add boiling water, and thicken with flour and water, after which boil well; season to taste with salt and pepper, and serve soup and vegetables separate; the meat will not be worth serving.

408. Potato Soup—With a small piece of salt pork and a little celery boil six peeled potatoes; strain or rub through a colander and add to it milk, butter and salt till of the consistency of cream; add some finely chopped parsley and boil all five minutes; cut some stale bread into dice, fry brown in hot lard and throw into the soup just before serving.—*Palmer House, Chicago.*

409. Hulled Corn Broth—Boil half a pint of white beans; when done pour off the water and add fresh; then put in lean salt pork or corned beef; when nearly done take hulled corn previously boiled separately and put into the broth; be sure to have plenty of water.

410. Gumbo Soup—Fry out the fat of a slice of bacon or fat ham, drain it off, and in it fry the slices of a large onion brown; scald, peel, and cut up two quarts fresh tomatoes, when in season (use canned tomatoes otherwise), and cut thin one quart okra; put them, together with a little chopped parsley, in a stew-kettle, with about three quarts water, and cook slowly two or three hours; season with salt and pepper before serving.

411. Chicken Soup—Save the broth after boiling chickens, and to it add a dozen fresh tomatoes, or a quart of canned, and an onion thinly sliced; boil twenty minutes, season with salt and pepper, add two beaten eggs, and serve.

The same quantity of okra pods used for thickening instead of tomatoes, forms a chicken gumbo soup.

412. Chicken Soup, with Rice—Put in a sauce-pan two old chickens, a small beef shank or other soup meat, one bunch soup greens, salt and a few whole peppers; cover with cold water and let it come to a slow boil; skim well when the chicken is done, strain the broth on one-half cup rice, let it cook slowly till done, then add the meat of one chicken cut fine and a little nutmeg, and serve.—*Palmer House, Chicago.*

413. Force Meat Balls for Mock Turtle, Meat or Game Soups—In a wedge-wood mortar rub the yelks of five hard-boiled eggs, or in a bowl with the back of a spoon, adding gradually some calves brains; mix in two eggs beaten lightly to moisten, and season with a little butter and salt. Put in the soup five minutes before serving.

WHOLESALE AND RETAIL.  NEAR MONROE STREET.

We carry the most varied and largest Retail Stock of Shelf Hardware in the City.

PARTICULAR ATTENTION GIVEN TO

BUILDERS' HARDWARE

Embracing all the Leading Makes of Fine Bronze Trimmings.

A Specialty made of Butchers' Tools & Machinery.

ORR & LOCKETT.

L. E. NELSON,

No. 70 North Clark Street,

DEALER IN

Ranges, Stoves & Heaters

Also full lines of Housekeeping Goods in Iron, Tin, Copper Ware, Cutlery and Shelf Hardware.

Oil Stoves of best make, and a new Gasoline Stove, perfectly non-explosive.

The "Perfection" Refrigerator and Ice Chest (all sizes).

COPPER, TINWARE AND STOVE REPAIRING.

OPEN EVENINGS.

JOHN ANDERSON'S

DEPOT FOR

Butter, Cheese & Eggs

OF RELIABLE QUALITY AND AT LOWEST PRICES.

Also the best article of Butterine made—sold as such, superior to Cheap Butter.

A CLEANLY AND LOW-PRICED RESTAURANT ADJOINING.

Nos. 11 & 13 South Clark Street, near South Water.

JOHN H. GRANT,

248 Wabash Ave., Chicago, Ill.,

MANUFACTURER AND DEALER IN

Sewing Machine Needles

→ OIL ←

Parts and Attachments.

New first-class Sewing Machines at $20 and upwards, and warranted for five years.

Good Second-Hand Machines at $5 and upwards.

Repairing all makes of Sewing Machines a specialty, and satisfaction guaranteed.

THE UNION FOLDING BED

CLOSED.

OPEN.

Gives a perfect Woven Wire Mattress Bed, and encloses all of the bedding.

There are no legs to turn down.
Bedding folds outward, giving perfect ventilation.
See it before buying any other.
For sale by Furniture Dealers.

$25.00 AND UPWARD.

Variety of Styles.

ALSO MANUFACTURERS OF

Woven Wire Mattresses

AND

IRON AND BRASS BEDSTEADS

OF ALL KINDS

Suitable for homes and public institutions.

Union Wire Mattress Co.

73 to 83 Erie St., Chicago.

Full Catalogue sent on application.

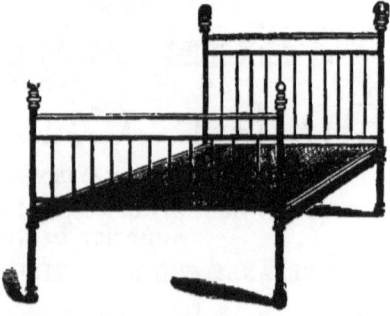

SALADS AND DRESSINGS.

Salads—*Note*—Salads vary so much in their ingredients and manner of mixing that they form not only a very agreeable relish, but frequently an entire meal. Great care should be taken that all vegetables entering into their composition should be very fresh, all meats, fowl or fish well cooked (except when they are directed raw), and that the vinegar be of the best quality, pure cider vinegar being the best attainable here, although the white wine or tarragon vinegars, when to be relied upon, are regarded as superior ; beware of acid vinegars so frequently palmed off as white wine vinegar. Prepare vegetables by freshening in cold water, and thoroughly cleansing. The oil used should be of the best and sweetest French or Italian olive oil, added a few drops at a time. For chicken salad the oil skimmed from the water in which the chicken is boiled may be used instead of salad oil, and as old fowls are really better than young for salads, this will be considerable. When the yelks of hard boiled eggs are used they should be mashed or pounded in a mortar or rubbed fine in a bowl with the back of a spoon; cream or clarified melted butter are a good substitute for oil, and by many preferred; it should be added last. To prepare lettuce, kale or cress, do not cut, but break off the heads or roots ; separate and wash each leaf separately, one by one, in water slightly warm or tepid, and immediately throw each one into cold water; the warmed water more effectually cleanses, while the cold water preserves the crispness. The meat from fowls or the bones of meat should also be picked off instead of cut. Vegetable salads should be stirred very little, that their freshness may be preserved.

414. Celery—To crisp celery let it lie in ice water two hours before serving; to fringe the stalks stick several coarse needles into a cork and draw the stalk half way from the top through the needles several times, and lay in the refrigerator to curl and crisp.

415. Chiccory or Endive—Extensively cultivated for the adulteration of coffee; is also a fine relish, and has broad leaves; endive is of the same nature as chiccory, the leaves being curly.

416. Cress or Water Cress—Is said to contain much sulphur and to be anti-scorbutic; it is of a peppery flavor, and when gathered early in the morning is a good breakfast appetizer; served simply with salt; it is also compounded into a salad.

417. Horse-Radish—Is an agreeable relish, and has a particularly fresh taste in the spring; is scraped fine or grated, and set on the table in a small covered cup; much that is bottled and sold as horse-radish is adulterated with grated turnip.

418. Lettuce—Wash each leaf separately, breaking them from the head; crisp in ice water and serve the leaves whole, to be prepared at table, providing hard boiled eggs cut in halves or slices, oil and other ingredients, to be mixed at table to individual taste.

419. Radishes—There are several varieties, all of which are served at table placed in a glass of water, having been previously cleaned by scraping.

420. Parsley—Is much used for flavoring in cookery; it is also added to some salads; that used for garnishing is known as the curly-head kind; it is best green and fresh, but may be dried for winter use; hang it in a dry place, the roots upwards.

421. Sorrel—Is found in a wild state in most localities; it possesses a certain amount of pure oxalic acid, which renders it a desirable concomitant for salad, and is regarded as very healthful.

422. Pepper Grass—Is of nearly the same nature as cress, and used in same manner.

423. Bean Salad—String young beans; break into half-inch pieces (or leave whole), wash and cook soft in salt water; drain well; add finely-chopped onions, pepper, salt and vinegar; when cool, add olive oil or melted butter.

424. Cabbage Salad—Two quarts finely-chopped cabbage, two level tablespoons salt, two of white sugar, one of black pepper, and a heaping one of ground mustard; rub yelks of four hard-boiled eggs until smooth; add half cup butter, slightly warmed; mix thoroughly with the cabbage, and add tea cup good vinegar; serve with whites of the eggs sliced and placed on the salad.

425. Plain Cold Slaw—Slice cabbage very fine; season with salt, pepper and a little sugar; pour over vinegar and mix thoroughly. It is nice served in the center of a platter with fried oysters around it.

426. Chicken Salad—Chop fine one chicken cooked tender, one head cabbage, and five cold hard-boiled eggs; season with salt, pepper and mustard to taste; warm one pint vinegar; add half a teacup butter; stir until melted; pour hot over the mixture; stir thoroughly, and set away to cool.

427. Chicken Salad—Two chickens; two bunches of celery to each chicken; half pint vinegar, two eggs, one tablespoon salad oil, one of liquid mustard, one of sugar, one of salt, one salt-spoon red pepper; beat the eggs and vinegar together until quite thick; then beat oil, mustard, and red pepper together, and stir into it; add celery just before using. The above is sufficient for ten persons.

428. Chicken Salad—Boil one chicken tender, and chop fine; chop fine the whites of twelve hard-boiled eggs; add equal quantities of chopped celery and cabbage; mash the yelks fine; add two tablespoons butter, two of sugar, one teaspoon mustard; pepper and salt to taste; and lastly, one-half cup good cider vinegar; pour over the salad and mix thoroughly.

429. Cucumber Salad—Peel and slice cucumbers; mix with salt, and let stand half an hour; mix two tablespoons sweet oil or ham gravy with as much vinegar and a teaspoon sugar; add the cucumbers, which should be drained a little; add a teaspoon pepper, and stir well.

430. Lettuce Salad—Take the yelks of three hard-boiled eggs, add salt and mustard to taste; mash fine; make a paste by adding a dessertspoon of olive oil or melted butter; mix thoroughly, and then dilute by adding gradually a tea cup of vinegar, and pour over the lettuce; garnish by slicing another egg and laying on top of the lettuce.

431. Lobster Salad—Put a large lobster over the fire in boiling water slightly salted; boil rapidly for about twenty minutes; when cold, crack the claws, after first disjointing, twist off the head (which is used in garnishing), split the body in two lengthwise, pick out the meat in bits not too fine, saving the coral separate; break up a large head of lettuce and place on a dish, over which lay the lobster, putting the coral around the outside; for dressing, take the yelks of three eggs, beat well, add four tablespoons salad oil, dropping it in very slowly, beating all the time; then add a little salt, cayenne pepper, half teaspoon mixed mustard and two tablespoons vinegar; pour this over the lobster just before sending to table.

432. Potato Salad, Hot—Pare six or eight large potatoes and boil till done, and slice thin while hot; peel and cut up a white onion into small bits and mix with the potatoes; cut up some breakfast bacon into small bits, sufficient to fill a tea cup, and fry it a light brown; remove the meat, and into the grease stir three tablespoons vinegar, making a sour gravy, which with the bacon pour over the potato and onion; mix lightly. To be eaten when hot.

433. Potato Salad, Cold—Chop cold boiled potatoes fine with enough raw onions to season nicely; make a dressing as for lettuce salad, and pour over it.

434. Cream Dressing for Cold Slaw—Two tablespoons whipped sweet cream, two of sugar, and four of vinegar; beat well and pour over cabbage.

435. Cabbage Salad Dressing—Boil one cup vinegar; melt a piece of butter the size of a walnut in it; beat together one egg and add one teaspoon each of mustard, sugar, salt, flour and half teaspoon pepper; pour the boiling vinegar on this mixture; stir it well; then put it back on the stove to boil again about a minute, and pour it over the cabbage.

436. Mayonaise Dressing—Beat a raw egg (some use the yelks only) with a salt-spoon of salt (using a wooden spoon) until it is thoroughly smooth; add a teaspoon mixed mustard, made rather thicker than usual; when quite smooth, add by degrees (a few drops only at a time) a half pint of salad oil, taking care to blend each portion of it with the egg before adding more. This ought to be as smooth as honey, and thick enough so that a spoon will stand up in it; dilute with vinegar until it assumes the consistency of thick cream. A little essence of anchovy may be added if desired. This is the smoothest and richest of salad dressings. The oily flavor is entirely lost in combination with the raw egg. This sauce keeps well, if bottled and corked with a glass stopper, and it may be made at any time in advance. In summer, place oil and eggs in a cold place half an hour before making.

MOODY & WATERS,

MANUFACTURERS OF

HOME-MADE PIES

Bakery: 216 & 218 W. Lake Street,
Office and Salesroom: 39 & 41 N. Green Street,

→CHICAGO.←

CAPACITY, 1,000 PIES PER HOUR.

When buying Pies call for the "HOME-MADE."
Our Pies are stamped "Home-Made" on the upper crust, and are always clean, well baked and manufactured of the best material that can be procured.
They are delivered fresh daily in all parts of the city, and are for sale by all Groceries, Bakeries, Restaurants and Confectioners.
N. B.—We use no cotton seed oil, glucose, corn starch or any article considered injurious to health.

EVERY AMERICAN CITIZEN

SHOULD HAVE A COPY OF

Babcock's Political Hand-Book

CONTAINING

Portraits and Biographies of 22 Leading Statesmen.
A History of all National Political Conventions ever held in the United States.

CABINETS OF ALL PRESIDENTS,

Justices of Supreme Court.
Losses of the Government by Embezzlement.
Popular and Electoral Votes, etc., etc.

128 pp. Price, Paper Covers, 25c.; in Cloth, 50c. For sale by the Trade.

BABCOCK, FORT & CO.

PUBLISHERS,
187 La Salle Street, Chicago.

PUDDINGS AND PASTRY.

Note—Upon the production of puddings and pastry, covering fruit pies, tarts and tartlets, the following general remarks are given. Most of those on cake making (page 95), will also apply here.

PUDDINGS.

Note—The freshness of all the ingredients for puddings is very essential, as one bad or poor article will taint the whole. When eggs are of doubtful freshness, break each one separately in a cup before mixing them ; a bad one will not then destroy those that preceded it. By beating the yelks and whites separately, the articles to which they are added will be the lighter.

Raisins and dried fruits for puddings should be carefully picked over, in most cases stoned, and large ones chopped. Currants should be well washed, pressed in a cloth, and then thoroughly dried before the fire, and after which be well picked over. English currants are usually quite gritty ; they may be made to "plump" or fill out by pouring over them boiling water, and then dried.

Batter pudding should be smoothly mixed, entirely free from lumps; to cause which, first mix the flour with a very small part of the milk, and add the remainder gradually; should it then prove lumpy, it may be rubbed through a hair sieve.

Boiled puddings should be put on in boiling water, which must not be allowed to stop at least simmering; it should always be covered with the water, more being added if necessary. In dishing it, as soon as it comes out of the kettle dip it in a pan of cold water, and the cloth will not stick to it. It is better to have them suspended in the kettle; the cloth will not then adhere to the bottom. The pudding cloth or bag should be kept scrupulously clean, but washed without soap, or they will impart a very disagreeable flavor to the puddings. Before using, dip in hot water and dredge it slightly with flour.

All puddings should be expeditiously served, as by standing they quickly become heavy, particularly batter puddings. When baked puddings are sufficiently solid to do so, turn them out of the baking-dish to a platter, bottom up, and powder with fine sugar.

437. Apple Pudding—One quart milk, three eggs, three teaspoons baking-powder, two spoonsful melted butter, flour to make a batter like griddle cakes; fill a pan half full of sliced apples, and pour the batter over them; bake two hours, and eat with a sweet sauce.

438. Apple Roley Poley—Peel, core and slice sour apples; make a rich biscuit dough, or raised biscuit dough may be used if rolled thinner; roll half an inch thick, lay the slices on the paste, roll up, tuck in the ends, prick deeply with a fork, lay it in a steamer, and steam hard for an hour and three-quarters. Or, wrap it in a pudding-cloth, tie the ends, baste up the sides, and boil continually an hour and a-half, perhaps more. Stoned cherries, dried fruits, or any kind of berries, fresh or dried, may be used.

439. Cabinet Pudding—Spread the inside of a plain mould with butter, and ornament the sides with dried cherries and candied citron; fill the mould with alternate layers of slices of sponge-cakes and ratafia of macaroni. Then fill up the mould with a lemon custard made with eight yelks of eggs, a pint of milk or cream, six ounces of sugar, a glass of brandy and the grated rind of a lemon. This custard must not be set, but merely mixed up. Steam the pudding in the usual way for about an hour and a-half, and when done dish it up, either with arrowroot sauce or a custard.—*Sebastien Michel, Chef de Cuisine, Hotel Brunswick.*

440. Corn Starch Blanc Mange—Take one quart sweet milk, and put one pint upon the stove to heat; in the other pint mix four heaping tablespoons corn starch; when the milk is hot, pour in the cold milk with the corn starch thoroughly mixed in it, and stir all together until there are no lumps and it is thick; flavor with lemon; take from the stove, and add the whites of three eggs beaten to a stiff froth.

A Custard for the Above.—One pint milk boiled with a little salt in it; beat the yelks of three eggs with half a cup of sugar, and add to the boiling milk; stir well, but do not let it boil till the eggs are put in.

441. English Plum Pudding—Beat six yelks and four whites of eggs very light, add to them a tumbler of sweet milk, stir in gradually a quarter pound grated stale bread, a pound of flour, three-quarters of sugar, and a pound each of beef suet chopped fine, currants nicely washed and dried, and stoned raisins well floured; stir well and add two nutmegs, a tablespoon mace, one of cinnamon or cloves, a wine glass brandy, a teaspoonful salt, and, finally, another tumbler milk; boil in bowls or moulds five hours, and serve with a sauce made with drawn butter, wine, sugar and nutmeg. It will keep several months; when wanted, boil an hour before serving; a pound of citron or blanched sweet almonds will add to the richness of the pudding.

442. Rice Pudding without Eggs—Two quarts milk, two-thirds of a cup of rice, same of sugar, and a small piece of butter and a little salt; stir it occasionally until boiling hot, and cook in a slow oven until of the consistency of cream.

443. A Cheap but Delicious Rice Pudding—One cup rice, well washed, two quarts new milk, a pinch of salt, with sugar and flavoring to taste; grate nutmeg over it, and bake in a slow oven four or five hours. This will prove a most delicious pudding, to be eaten either hot or cold, and if baked slowly is better than with the use of eggs.

444. Rice Meringue Pudding—Put a teacup of rice in a pint of water. When the water is boiled away, add a pint of milk, a piece of butter the size of an egg; the yelks of three eggs, and the grated rind of one lemon; mix well; pour into a pudding dish; spread over the top the whites of the eggs beaten to a stiff froth with a teacup of sugar; set in the oven and brown a little.

445. Plain Fruit Pudding—Take one and a-half cups of flour, one cup of bread crumbs, one cup of raisins, half a cup of currants, two nutmegs, one cup of suet chopped fine, two tablespoons of sugar, four eggs, a wine glass of brandy, a wine glass of syrup, and a little milk if necessary. Mix very thoroughly; tie it in a cloth as tight as possible, and boil fast for five or six hours. Serve with wine sauce.

446. Snow Pudding—One-half a package of Cox's gelatine; pour over it a cup of cold water, and add one and a-half cups sugar; when soft, add one cup boiling water and the juice of one lemon; then the whites of four well-beaten eggs; beat all together until it is light and frothy, or until the gelatine will not settle clear in the bottom of the dish after standing a few minutes; put it on a glass dish, and serve with a custard made of one pint milk, the yelks of the four eggs, and the grated rind of a lemon; boil.

447. Suet Pudding—Four cups flour, one cup molasses, one cup suet chopped fine, half-pound raisins, three-quarters of a cup milk, half teaspoon soda, and a little salt and cinnamon; boil two hours and a-half. To be eaten with sauce.

448. Sweet Pudding—Four cups flour, one of molasses, one of suet finely chopped, half-pound raisins, three-quarters of a cup of milk, half a teaspoon soda, and a little cinnamon; boil two hours and a half; serve with sauce.

•449. Yorkshire Pudding, with Roast Beef—See No. 97.

PASTRY.

The flour should be the best wheaten flour and perfectly dry, at least three months old; some brands of flour are especially in favor for pastry, among them the kind known as the "New Process." If in the least damp it will be heavy.

The butter, unless fresh is used, should be washed from the salt and well squeezed or wrung in a cloth to get out all the water or buttermilk; if left in, it will produce heavy paste.

Lard should be perfectly sweet and white. It may be tested by running a knife or steel into; if, on withdrawing, it smells sweet, it is good.

Suet should be finely chopped, perfectly sweet and free from skin-like tissue; when chopped, dredge with flour, which prevents the particles adhering to each other. Beef suet is the best, but that of veal, or the outside fat of a loin or neck of mutton, makes good shortening, or the skimmings from boiled mutton, but only that without vegetables. Clarified beef drippings also make good crusts for ordinary puddings, pies or cakes; it should, however, be used sparingly.

The art of making paste requires much practice and dexterity; it should be touched as lightly as possible, made with cool hands and in a cool place, and for same reason a marble slab is better than a board to knead or roll upon, using a well-floured rolling-pin of hard wood. In mixing, add the water (ice water is best in summer); very gradually work the whole together with the blade of a knife. The butter or other shortening should be cold and rather hard; to make it so put in cold water until about ready for it, when squeeze as before directed, break it in small bits, roll out the paste and cover with the bits of butter; fold over each end and roll out very thin again, repeating until all is used. To produce light pastes considerable expedition should be used both in making and baking; if it stands long before putting in the oven it will become flat and heavy.

In baking custard, pumpkin or squash pies, that the mixture may not be absorbed by the paste, it is better to partly bake the crust before adding it.

The pie tins, patty pans or dishes for baked puddings should be well greased, ready for use, sweet lard being as good or preferable to butter; crusts to be baked in sheets should be placed on buttered paper.

Oven—Very important is the state of the oven; if a paste be skillfully compounded with the best materials, and not properly baked, all is lost. Some require a quick oven, as puff-paste; others a warm and moderate one, and some a slow one. By placing a hand in the oven its heat may be determined very nearly. In baking a puff-paste try a small piece of the paste first.

450. Puff Paste—One full pound sifted superfine flour, one of washed butter, pressed free from moisture in a clean cloth; place the flour on the mixing board or marble slab; make a well in the center, into which squeeze the juice of half a lemon, and put in the yelk of an egg, beaten with a little ice-water; stir with one hand and drop in ice-water with the other until the paste is hard as the butter; roll out the paste in a smooth square an inch thick; smooth the sides with a rolling-pin and spread the butter over half the paste; lay the other half over it, and leave it for fifteen minutes in a cold place; then roll out in a long strip, keeping the edges smooth, and double it in three parts, thus: lap one-third over the middle, roll it down, then fold over the opposite third, and roll all out in a long strip again; repeat the folding, rolling across this time; let it lie fifteen minutes, and repeat six times, allowing fifteen minutes between each rolling to cool, or the butter will oil; the paste is now ready for use. The result will repay the trouble by being both light and flaky. The quantity of water depends on the capacity of the flour to absorb it. Handle as little as possible throughout the whole process. Rich pastes such as the above require a quick oven.

451. Patties or Shells for Tarts—Roll out a nice puff paste thin; cut out with a glass or cookie cutter, and with a wine glass or smaller cutter cut out the center of two out of three; lay the rings thus made on the third, and bake at once. May be used for veal or oyster patties, or filled with any jelly, jam or preserves as tarts.

452. Apple Custard Pie—Stew sour apples until soft and not much water is left in them, and rub through a colander; beat three eggs for each pie, and use one cup butter and one of flour for three pies; nutmeg seasoning.

453. Apple Tarts—Pare, quarter, core and boil in half a cup water until quite soft ten large, tart apples; beat until very smooth and add the yelks of six eggs or three whole ones, the juice and grated outside rind of two lemons, half a cup butter, one and a-half of sugar (or more if not sufficiently sweet); beat all thoroughly, line patty pans with a puff paste and fill; bake five minutes in a hot oven.

Meringue—If desired very nice, cover them when removed from the oven with a meringue made of the whites of the three eggs remaining, mixed with three tablespoons sugar; return to the oven and delicately brown.

454. Cream Pie—Thoroughly beat together half a cup sugar, the white of one egg and a tablespoon flour; then add a cup of rich milk, or use part cream; bake with only an undercrust, and grate nutmeg over it.

455. Date Pie—One pound of dates makes three pies; soak them over night, then stew them until soft enough to strain; add one quart milk, three eggs, a little nutmeg and salt; bake without an upper crust.

456. Lemon Pie—Grate the yellow rind and take the juice of one lemon, one cup sugar; take a heaping tablespoon of corn-starch and mix it with cold water; add a cup of boiling water, and cook a little; turn together; beat the yelk of one egg, and add to the mixture; beat the whites of two eggs to a froth with a little sugar, and put over the top after the pie is baked, and set in the oven to slightly brown.

457. Lemon Pie—Into one quart boiling molasses put one-half cup water, the grated rind and juice of six lemons, one large spoonful corn starch, and two beaten eggs. This will fill three pies.

458. Mince Meat—Use two bowls chopped apples, one of chopped meat, one-fourth pound chopped suet, the grated rind and juice of one lemon, two tea cups molasses, one large teaspoon each of cinnamon and cloves, one nutmeg grated fine, one pound stoned or seedless raisins, half pound currants, one-fourth pound citron cut fine, one quart cider, and sugar and salt to taste.

459. Mock Mince Pie—Twelve crackers rolled fine, one cup hot water, half cup of vinegar, one cup each of sugar, currants and raisins; any spices to taste. This makes four pies.

460. Pumpkin Pie—For three pies: one quart milk, three cups of boiled and strained pumpkin, one and a-half cups sugar, one-half cup molasses, four eggs, a little salt, and one teaspoon each of ginger and cinnamon. Boston marrow or Hubbard squash may be substituted for pumpkin, and are much preferred by many, as possessing a less strong flavor.

BREMNER'S
D. F. B.
EUREKA BREAD

This Bread is made with the Best Minnesota Patent Flour ground from wheat selected for this purpose, with Milk from my own dairy farm, which is absolutely pure and full cream. The dough is mixed by machinery, made under my own directions from my own designs, and my patrons can see that it must be a much *cleaner and uniform bread* than that which is mixed up by hands.

Purity of Material, Superiority of Workmanship and Cleanliness in Handling are my mottoes.

FINE BISCUIT & FAMILY CRACKERS

Are as much superior to other brands as my Bread.

SNOW FLAKE, SODA & CREAM WAFERS

In tin cans, are not excelled.

See that your Grocer gives you **BREMNER'S** goods.

CAKE🞉CONFECTIONERY.

Of the numberless cakes produced through the multiferous combinations of flour, sugar, fruits, raising powders or other ingredients, those only will be presented which lie within the skill of the accomplished housekeeper. Ornamentation and decoration of fine cakes will be but lightly touched upon; it is a part, however, which presents an opportunity for the display of much taste and skill on the part of the operator.

Preliminary Matters to Observe in Cake Making—Clean hands and nails thoroughly with a brush. Clean all utensils and the kitchen table very thoroughly, and have everything necessary in readiness. If the weather is warm place the eggs in a cold place, as they will beat stiffer and lighter; examine each thoroughly to ascertain if they are sound and fresh. Prepare the tins before the cake is made, greasing with lard, and line the bottom with several thicknesses of paper, the top one well greased; it will do no harm to also line the sides.

All flour and sugar used is to be sifted and weighed. Very hard butter should be warmed a little, but not melted. If quite salt or packed butter, freshen in cold water, breaking it into bits. None but "*good butter*" should ever be used, and if beaten to a cream it saves warming. In using milk observe that with sour milk soda alone is necessary, but with sweet milk soda and cream of tartar or baking powder is used; the first makes a spongy, light cake, and the last one like pound cake.

For all white and delicate cakes use powdered sugar; for rich cakes, plum cake, crushed loaf, powdered and sifted; for dark cakes, the best brown sugar, and for jelly cakes, light fruit cakes, "A" coffee or granulated.

New flour in either bread or cake making, or for pastry, may be improved, *i. e.*, some of its moisture evaporated—by placing in the sun or before the fire the quantity to be used. When using "New Process" flour recollect it requires less by an eighth than any other brand.

Most good cake makers first stir the milk and flavoring into the creamed butter and sugar, then the yelks, next the whites and last the flour, after first mixing with two-thirds of it the baking powder, leaving the remainder to be used at discretion.

A cup always means a tea-cup, and not a coffee-cup.

Raisins should not be washed; to remove all dirt, stems, etc., rub them in a cloth and then carefully pick them over; if washed, it is difficult to dry them, so they will not make the cake heavy. Raisins or other fruit should be added the last thing before the cake is baked. Grate only the outer or yellow rind of lemons or oranges; the white or inner peel contains none of the required flavor, but, on the contrary, is bitter A reliable baking powder may be used in all cases where soda and cream of tartar is mentioned, using the same quantity given for the two together. The proportions to use of baking powder is generally three teaspoons to a quart of flour, or one of soda and two of cream of tartar.

Do not stir, but beat cake batter, beating upward and very thoroughly; beat with a wooden spoon; iron will turn the batter dark, and for same reason always use an earthen or stoneware vessel to beat it in.

The proper heating of the oven is of great importance, especially for large cakes; if not very hot the batter will not rise. If the oven be too quick, and there is danger of burning, put a sheet of clean white paper over the top.

To ascertain when a cake is properly done stick a knife or knitting-needle to the center, withdraw it quickly, and if it looks at all sticky it is not and must be returned.

It is better to keep cake in a closed tin cake-box or covered jar, and always in a dry place.

461. Coldwater Pound Cake—Half cup butter, two of sugar, three eggs, one cup cold water, three pounds flour, one teaspoon cream tartar, one-half teaspoon soda.

462. Cocoanut Cookies—One cup sugar, half cup butter, one egg, two tablespoons milk, one and a-half teaspoons baking powder, and a little salt, one cup desiccated or grated cocoanut, enough flour to roll.

463. Delicious Cake—One cup sugar, half cup butter, two eggs—the yelks and whites separately beaten—half a cup milk, one cup and a-half flour, and one and a-half teaspoons baking powder.

464. French Chocolate Cake—The whites of seven eggs two cups sugar, two-thirds cup butter, one of milk and three of flour, three teaspoons baking powder; the chocolate part of the cake is made the same as the above, only use yelks of the eggs and one cup grated chocolate; bake it in layers, and spread a custard between them, which is made with two eggs, one pint milk, one-half cup sugar, one tablespoon corn-starch, and one teaspoon extract vanilla.

465. Jumbles—Two cups sugar, one of butter, three eggs, one-third cup of milk, one and a-half teaspoons baking powder, and flour enough to roll.

466. Lemon Cake—One and a-half cups sugar, half cup butter, three eggs, half teaspoon soda dissolved in half cup of milk, two heaping cups sifted flour, a little salt, and the grated peel and juice of one lemon; bake in two shallow pans, and cut into squares.

467. Lemon Snaps—One cup sugar, one-half cup butter, two eggs, one teaspoon essence lemon, a quarter teaspoon soda dissolved in a teaspoon of milk, flour enough to make very stiff, and roll very thin.

468. Marble Cake—*For the White Part*—Half cup butter, one and a-half cups white sugar, half a cup sweet milk, two and a-half pounds flour, a quarter teaspoon soda, the whites of four eggs; flavor with lemon.

For the Dark Part—Half cup butter, the same of molasses, two of brown sugar, half cup sour milk, half teaspoon soda, yelks of four eggs, and one whole egg, two cups flour, spices to taste; after each part is thoroughly mixed, butter the pans well and put in first a couple of large spoons of the dark, and then the same of white part, alternately, until all is used.

469. Molasses Gingerbread—One large cup molasses, one tablespoon lard, one cup sour milk, a dessert spoon soda, one tablespoon ginger, and flour to make a very stiff paste.

470. Neapolitaines—One pound of flour, half pound of powdered sugar, half pound of butter, six eggs, six yelks, quarter ounce of rose or orange blossom water; mix the flour, sugar, butter and eggs together with the perfume; if too stiff, add a little milk; leave the dough half an hour in a cool place; roll it out a quarter of an inch thick, and cut it with a small tin cutter of any shape; put the cakes on a pan slightly greased, and color the tops with beaten egg and milk, with some chopped almonds over them; cook in a very hot oven.—*Fernand Fere, Chef de Cuisine, Astor House, New York.*

471. Spice Cake—One cup sugar, a piece of butter the size of an egg, one egg, one cup sour milk, one teaspoon soda; spice to taste, and flour enough to make a thick batter.

472. Sponge Cake—The desirable feature of good sponge cake is its lightness, which is only attained by long-continued hard beating, to do this well requires two persons. While one beats the yelk for fifteen to twenty minutes, as light and creamy as possible, and then beats in three-quarters of a pound of sugar with rose water until thick and light, another person should beat the whites until well frothed, but do not whiten, then slowly beat into them the remaining quarter pound of sugar, and whisk until it no longer stiffens, or until the former preparation is complete. Now, lightly and steadily add the last mixture and the flour with the first, a little of each alternately, stirring only enough to mix them well, avoiding hard beating which would toughen the whole. The buttered pans should be ready, and whether round, square or patty pans, fill them half to two-thirds full; sift sugar over them, and bake in a moderate oven. Material: Ten ounces of sifted pastry flour, a pound powdered sugar, twelve eggs, two tablespoons rose water, or other flavors may be used, as almonds, using an ounce blanched bitter almonds; lemon, use the grated rind and juice of two large lemons, mixed and strained after standing an hour; vanilla, use a tablespoon of vanilla sugar, beat in with the yelks at first—the two others mix with the sugar. The cake may be iced with rose icing or with almond, orange-flower, lemon or vanilla icing. This is a very useful cake in the formation of the different *Charlottes* jelly cakes, lady-fingers, or in small round cup cakes.

473. Sponge Cake—Two cups sugar, five eggs, two-thirds cup boiling water, two and a-half cups flour, two teaspoons baking powder; beat the yelks of the eggs thin; add the sugar; when well beaten together add the boiling water, then the whites which have been beaten to a stiff froth, and lastly the flour and baking powder; flavor with lemon or vanilla.

474. Cream Frosting—A cup of sweet cream whipped and flavored with vanilla, cut a loaf of cake in two, spread the frosting between and on the top; this tastes like Charlotte Russe.

475. Hard or Plain Icing for Cake—Break the whites of four eggs into a large platter, in a cool room, or in summer set it on ice; whisk them until they foam, but do not whiten; then sift in the sugar slowly, beating steadily from the bottom, so as to bring up every drop at each sweep of the whip, and continue until as white and fine as snow and can be cut with a knife.

If the whites do not froth, throw in a pinch of alum or soda; sometimes they may require a little more sugar, but the average is four ounces to the white of a full-sized egg. This is a plain icing. All icings should be applied in two coats; let the first one dry before putting on the second, which can be sufficiently thinned with water to work smooth. If any ornaments are used, they must be put on while the second icing is still moist. The flavors mostly used are almond, chocolate, lemon, orange, rose or vanilla.

476. A Soft Icing—Is preferable to hard for some kinds of cake. Mix half a pound of finely pulverized and sifted sugar with a tablespoon boiling water, and the same of any fruit juices fancied; spread at once on the cake while yet warm, about an eighth of an inch thick; color if desired.

CONFECTIONERY.

We give only such plain home-made candies as are easily produced.

Most kitchens will possess utensils which may be used in candy-making, one of the most convenient of which is a block tin sauce-pan, with flaring sides, a long handle, and a lip to facilitate pouring; or a porcelain, iron or brass kettle will do, but should be very clean. Make candies in a vessel deep enough to contain it when swelled by heat, and remove from the fire when danger of boiling over. Watch carefully that it does not burn.

477. Clarifying Syrup—Dissolve four pounds white sugar in a quart of water, place over a slow fire for half an hour and stir in the white of an egg; skim off all impurities that arise, or dissolve together a small quantity of gelatine and gum-arabic and pour in instead of the egg. To perfect the clarification still more strain it through a jelly bag.

478. Other Candies—Are produced from the same syrup by bringing it to such a heat that the threads which drop from the spoon, when exposed to cold air, will be brittle and snap like glass. When this stage is reached add a teaspoon of vinegar or cream tartar to prevent graining. It may then be flavored, colored, poured into pans or pulled into sticks. To make into sticks pull or roll into shape, with the hands greased or floured.

479. Rock Candy—Boil the above much longer; allow it to cool, and the crystallization will form at the sides of the kettle or adhere to threads hung in it.

480. Butter Scotch—Three pounds "A" coffee sugar, a quarter pound butter, half teaspoon cream tartar, eight drops extract lemon; add sufficient water only to dissolve the sugar; boil without stirring till it will easily break when dropped in cold water, and when done add the lemon; pour into a well buttered dripping-pan a quarter inch thick, and when partly cold mark off into small squares.

481. Ice Cream Candy—Make the candy as above, flavoring with vanilla, rose or lemon, and when partly cold pull until very white. It may also be colored to a pink color with a little carmine.

482. Chocolate Caramels—One and a-half cups grated chocolate, four of brown sugar, one and a-half cold water, an egg-sized piece of butter and two tablespoons sharp vinegar; boil on the top of a stove over a brisk fire until it becomes brittle when dropped in water; do not stir, but shake the vessel while boiling; flavor with two tablespoons vanilla just before taking from the fire; pour into a buttered and floured dripping-pan, and check off into even squares while soft.

483. Cocoa-Nut Drops—One pound desiccated cocoa-nut, half pound powdered sugar and the white of an egg; work all together, roll into little balls in the hand and bake on buttered tins.

484. Hickory Nut Macaroons—To hickory nuts pounded fine add mixed ground allspice and nutmeg; make a frosting as for cakes; stir in the meats and spices, putting in enough only to make it convenient to handle; flour the hands, and make the mixture into balls about the size of a nutmeg; lay them on tins well buttered, giving room to spread; bake in a quick oven; use washed butter for greasing the tins; lard or salt butter gives an unpleasant taste.

485. Hoarhound Candy—Boil two ounces dried hoarhound in a pint and a-half water for about half an hour, strain and add three and a half pounds brown sugar; boil over a hot fire until sufficiently hard; pour out in flat, well greased tins and mark into sticks or small squares with a knife as soon as cool enough to retain its shape.

486. Molasses Candy—One cup molasses (common or New Orleans), one cup sugar, an egg-sized piece of butter sweet and not salt, and a tablespoon vinegar; boil, but do not stir until it hardens when dropped into cold water; when done stir in a teaspoon of soda and beat well; pour into buttered pans, and when cool pull until white; cut into sticks; flavor if desired, just before pouring out to cool.

487. Caramel or Burnt Sugar—*For Coloring Soups, Sauces or Gravies*—Put one cup sugar and two teaspoons water in a saucepan on the fire; stir constantly until it is quite a dark color, then add a half cup water and a pinch of salt; let it boil a few minutes, and when cold, bottle.

→ICE CREAM.←

WM. THOMPSON,

Manufacturer of Pure

ICE CREAMS AND ICES

AND WHOLESALE DEALER IN

→Milk and Cream.←

I make a specialty of Dining Cars, Hotels, Restaurants, Picnics, Church Festivals, Dealers, etc.

Being the largest manufacturer in the West and the second in the United States, and affording better facilities than other manufacturers, by owning my own milk dairy, raising my own cream, owning four farms stocked with cows, which produce 100 cans of milk daily, and being the largest milk dealer in the city, I feel justified in guaranteeing to my patrons better goods for the same money than any other dealer.

Goods delivered in city free of charge.

Again soliciting your valued patronage, I am, very respectfully, yours,

WM. THOMPSON,
154 Dearborn St., Chicago, Ill.

P. S.—Country orders will receive prompt attention. Special rates to dealers.

CUSTARDS, CREAMS & ICES.

Note—The preparation of these delicacies successfully is a matter of considerable care and attention to detail, and the following condensed directions are necessary:

A custard-kettle is almost indispensable, but one may be improvised by setting a tin pail within a kettle or sauce-pan; it is made of block tin or tinned iron, one within the other, forming a water-bath. Gelatine used for creams should be soaked for an hour or so in a little cold water or milk set in a warm place; a bowl set in the top of a tea kettle will be most convenient. Use it by pouring into the hot custard just after removing from the fire. For creams or custards, eggs should be beaten in stone or earthenware to attain the creamy lightness desirable. For custards, the usual rule is four eggs, a cup sugar, and a saltspoon of salt to a quart of milk. Bake in a baking-dish until firm in the center, taking care that the heat is but moderate, or it will turn mostly to whey; it will thus be much more delicate. For boiled custards, the yelks alone should be used, but for economy, the whole egg; boil the milk in the custard-kettle, and when, by a light foam on top, it shows to be about boiling, add the sugar; let it remain a few minutes, stirring until it thickens a little, but not long enough to curdle, then immediately set the inner kettle (or pail, if not a custard-kettle) in cold water, or at once turn out into a cold dish; curdling will result from its standing in the kettle. Boiled custards require the closest attention until finished. A box-wood or heavily tinned iron spoon, with a long handle, should be used for custards or creams.

The moulds for *Charlotte Russe*, blanc mange, and all other creams should be first wet with cold water before setting on the ice to harden. Gelatine is not necessary for *Charlotte Russe;* the filling may be made stiff enough by using an egg whip or beater, or whip churn, for the purpose.

488. Ice Creams—*Note*—There are two entire different and distinct kinds produced by confectioners or professional caterers in this country, one known as *Neapolitan* (originally produced at Naples, in Italy), and the *Philadelphia*, originating in that city. The former contains a greater proportion of eggs, and is rich, smooth and solid as butter, is a lemon yellow color and custard flavor. The latter has the full, rich flavor of sweet cream, and of a creamy white tint.

489. *The Materials* for ice cream are principally cream, sugar, eggs, all varieties of flavors, fruit and their juices, ice and salt; also may be added different colorings.

490. *The Cream*—Regarding cream, it may be said here that it can have no substitute, either by dilution with part milk, or milk and either tapioca, arrowroot, corn-starch or the addition of gelatine; the production will not be *ice cream*, but a *frozen milk custard*. The first operation is the cooking of the cream and sugar, with or without eggs, according to the kind, Neapolitan or Philadelphia, desired.

491. *For Neapolitan Ice Cream*—Strain and beat the yelks to a smooth cream, add the sugar and again beat; strain and whisk the whites to the stiffest possible froth, and stir briskly with the yelks and sugar; then mix with the cream, adding such flavors as are needed to be cooked. Cook the whole in a custard-kettle over a brisk fire, stirring continually until it will slightly coat the blade of a knife, but does not run; then be careful it does not curdle. Take it off the fire and strain through a wire sieve into a crockeryware bowl; cover it with a gauze and let it cool; pour it into the freezer (which should be of at least six quarts capacity), and set it in the ice pail or tub, well pack it with ice, and let it stand, covered only with gauze, until thoroughly cold, when it is ready for freezing.

492. *For Philadelphia Ice Cream*—It is sometimes made from uncooked cream, if fresh, and if desired of a very light or snowy texture, this is better, but must be beat, during its entire freezing, vigorously. It will swell or increase in bulk from a quarter to a third, but loses in quality, and consequently the cooking is preferable, giving it greater body and richness. Cook it in a custard-kettle, as previously directed, until the water in the outer pan boils, take it off the fire, add the sugar and any flavors that may be cooked with it, stir until the sugar is entirely dissolved, let stand a few minutes, strain and cool same as the Neapolitan. Fruit juices are not to be cooked with cream in any case, but mixed with the sugar; stir until a clear syrup is produced, and stirred into the ice cold cream before commencing to freeze it; or better, beaten into it just after it is frozen. In attempting to freeze cream when even lukewarm, it is apt to curdle or become granulated; it is also more rapidly and easily frozen if first chilled, and with less ice.

493. *The Freezer*—For family use, select one of the new patent freezers, as being more rapid and less laborious for small quantities than the old style turned entirely by the hand. All conditions being perfect, those with crank and revolving dashers effect freezing in eight to fifteen minutes.

494. *Freezing*—Take the freezer containing the ice cream, as above, from the ice-pail, remove the ice and water; replace the freezer and pack with ice nearly to the brim, sprinkling a quart of coarse salt uniformly through it as it is put in; cover and fasten the can and turn the crank until difficult to turn longer; open the can, remove the dasher, scrape the hardened cream from the sides with a spatula, and beat the contents with a wooden paddle till smooth, but no longer; close the can, draw off the salt brine into a bucket; add fresh salt and ice, covering also the top; wrap a blanket or piece of carpet around and over the ice-pail; wet it well with icy brine and let stand for an hour and a-half to two hours; open the freezer, scrape down and beat the cream again, and again pack with fresh ice and salt to harden and ripen. Be very careful not to let a drop of brine or a grain of salt get into the cream. In very warm weather it may be necessary to renew the ice and salt a second or third time; it should always be done whenever the brine floats the ice. All the directions being followed no better ice cream can be produced.

495. Water Ices—*Note*—Are all compounded of the juice of fruit, sugar and water. For the reason that they are generally produced in texture like a hardened mixture of flavored snow and water, often lumpy and having a gritty taste, they enjoy less popularity than ice creams. They melt quickly, even in the freezing can, if left open but a few minutes, and soon become soft and spongy. Water ices are made of many degrees of richness, from the pure juice of fruit, with its weight of sugar, down to a simple frozen lemonade.

By observing the following directions they may be made as smooth and firm as the best ice cream.

496. *General Instructions for Producing in every Variety*—The sugar and water must be cooked in a custard-kettle to a clear syrup, the scum removed and then strained through a fine muslin cloth and set to cool; pour it into the freezer, add the prepared fruit juices and other materials, if any, and pack with ice in lumps the size of an egg, sprinkling in a quart of coarse salt as it is added; cover and fasten the can, and turn slowly and steadily until it goes rather hard. It requires more time for freezing than for ice creams, generally fifteen to twenty minutes.

Open the can, scrape down the sides, and stir till smooth; then put in the white of one egg, beaten with a teaspoon of finely powdered sugar, to a stiff froth, and worked smooth; a larger quantity of egg is apt to produce a milky appearance.

Then proceed as for ice cream at this stage, letting it stand longer, two to three hours. Always keep the blanket wet with the icy brine.

If the granular kind of ices are desired, mix the sugar, water and juices, and freeze without cooking; also omit the egg finish.

When fruit jellies are used, gently heat the water sufficiently to melt them, then cool and freeze as above directed.

497. Moulding—Ice creams and water ices are moulded in same manner. The moulds should be filled solidly in every part, to expel all air; heap the cream a little above the brim, press the cover down hard, bind a buttered cloth over the joint, and bury it in ice and salt. If the mould be a figure in two parts, fill each half a little more than full; the excess will squeeze out on closing. When ready to serve, wash the moulds in cold water, take off the cloth, wipe the mould dry, lift off the cover, and turn it over on a plate; if the room is warm it will slip off the cream in a few minutes. Never immerse or use warm water.

498. Granites or "Frappes"—Turn them out as soon as half frozen, like wet snow.

Six quarts of the following are produced by this process:

499. Orange Ice—Three quarts water, four pounds sugar, one quart orange juice and juice of two lemons; requires a dozen and a half juicy oranges. Lemon, strawberry or raspberry made in same manner, using the fruit juices or extracts.

500. Pineapple Ice—Water and sugar as above; one and a-half pints pineapple, a gill orange, and half a gill lemon juices; requires two large pines, six oranges and three lemons. The pineapple juice is prepared thus: Select bird's-eye pines, take out the core or heart, which is bitter; mash and strain the pulp, using immediately, as it quickly darkens,

PRUSSING'S
→APPLE←
VINEGAR

AN ABSOLUTELY PURE ARTICLE,

MADE OF

Clarified Cider & Malt Spirits

Combining the Fruity Flavor of the Apple, with the Preserving Quality of a Malt Vinegar.

The Only Reliable Vinegar For Pickling!

Every Barrel Labeled with our Written Guarantee of its Absolute Purity and Preserving Qualities. Housekeepers should insist on getting

PRUSSING'S APPLE VINEGAR

If they want their Pickles kept Crisp and Firm for Years.

First Premiums Awarded at United States, Illinois State, and Chicago City Fairs.

Prussing Vinegar Co.
CHICAGO.

SAUCES, CATSUPS & PICKLES.

Sauces—*Note*—Not the least in importance in the art of cookery are sauces. Many an excellent piece of meat or fowls are spoiled by using a bad, inappropriate or indifferent sauce; while, on the other hand, good sauces add much to the delicacy of food preparations. In nothing is there a wider or a better field for the display of the talent or taste of the cook than in their skillful production or adaptability. Contrary to an erroneous but prevailing opinion, good sauces or gravies are quite easily and inexpensively produced. They should all be decided in character, and whether sweet, piquant, savory or plain, should maintain their name by their flavor.

The basis of most sauces or gravies is the same as for soups—the " stock kettle " (see note on SOUPS, page 81).

Being usually served in smaller quantities than soups, and as they should be served very hot, they require the special care of the cook. Those sauces formed in part of cream or eggs should be well stirred from the time they are added, and while kept very hot, to prevent curdling, should never be allowed to boil. As a rule they should be added last, or just before serving. Stir soups, sauces or catsups with a wooden spoon, never a metal one.

501. Anchovy Sauce—Add two teaspoons of anchovy paste or essence—kept by all first-class grocers—to white sauce, No. 515, or drawn butter, No. 507. It should be served with or upon boiled fish, especially boiled cod.

502. Apple Sauce—Made plain, simply stewing and sweetening, adding a little cinnamon or nutmeg, or both; is usually served with roast pork or goose.

503. Caper or Nasturtion Sauce—*For Boiled Mutton*—Chop the capers a very little, unless quite small; make half a pint drawn butter, to which add the capers, with a large spoon of the juice from the bottle in which they are sold; let it just simmer, and serve in a tureen. Nasturtions much resemble capers in taste, though larger, and may be used, and, in fact, are preferred by many. They are grown on a climbing vine, and are cultivated for their blossom and for pickling. When used as capers they should be chopped more. If neither capers or nasturtions are at hand some pickled gherkins, chopped up, form a very good substitute in the sauce.

504. Chili Sauce—Take twelve large ripe tomatoes, four ripe or three green peppers, two onions, two tablespoons salt, two of sugar, one of cinnamon, three cups vinegar; peel tomatoes and onions; chop them separately very fine; add the peppers chopped with the other ingredients, and boil one and a-half hours. A quart of canned tomatoes may be used instead of the ripe ones, when out of season

505. Chili Sauce—Use twenty-six medium-sized ripe tomatoes, two onions, four peppers—one green—chopped fine, two cups vinegar, two tablespoons salt, twelve tablespoons brown sugar, two of ginger, two of ground cinnamon, one of cloves, one of allspice, one nutmeg; boil gently about two hours; for larger quantities use same proportions.

506. Cranberry Sauce—After removing all imperfect or soft berries, wash thoroughly; place for about two minutes in scalding water; skim out or drain, and to every pound of fruit add three-quarters of a pound granulated sugar, a half pint water, and stew over a moderate fire. Be careful to cover, but don't stir the fruit, occasionally shaking the pan if in danger of burning. The berries will thus retain their shape and add to their appearance. Boil from five to seven minutes; remove from fire; turn into a deep dish, and set aside to cool. If to be kept, they can be put up in air-tight jars.

507. Drawn Butter—Into a half tablespoon of flour rub a small cup of butter; beat it very thoroughly until smooth; add a little salt if the butter does not afford enough, and pour on it half a pint boiling water, stirring fast; do not let it boil, or it will be oily, and consequently spoiled. It will be less likely to burn if prepared in a custard kettle or water bath. This resembles the white sauce, No. 515, and may be made to form the nucleus for a great variety of sauces for fish, poultry or boiled meats by the addition of different herbs; first throw them into boiling water, cut fine, and add.

508. Green Tomato Sauce—Cut up a pint of green tomatoes; take three gills black mustard seed, three tablespoons dry mustard, two and a-half of black pepper, one and a-half allspice, four of salt, two of celery seed, one quart each of chopped onions and sugar, and two and a-half quarts good vinegar, a little red pepper to taste; beat the spices and boil all together until well done.

509. Lemon Sauce—Cut three slices of lemon into very small dice, and put them into drawn butter; let it come just to boiling point, and pour over boiled fowls.

510. Lobster Sauce—Chop the meat from the claws and tail of a good sized lobster into pieces, but not too small, and half an hour before dinner make half a pint drawn butter or white sauce and mix.

511. Mayonnaise Sauce—In hot weather it may be necessary to place the bowl over ice in preparing it; in a two-quart bowl mix one even teaspoon ground mustard, one of salt and one and a-half of vinegar; beat in the yelk of a raw egg, then add very gradually half a pint pure olive oil or clarified butter, beating briskly all the time; the mixture will become a very thick batter; flavor with vinegar or fresh lemon juice; when closely covered it will keep for some weeks in a cold place.

512. Mint Sauce—The mint usually employed is spearmint, although peppermint for convenience is sometimes used. Take fresh, young mint, strip leaves from stems, wash, drain on a sieve or dry them on a cloth; chop very fine, put in a sauce-tureen, and to three heaped tablespoons mint add two of powdered sugar; let remain a few minutes well mixed together, and pour over it gradually six tablespoons of good vinegar; the sauce may be strained after it has stood for two or three hours, pressing it well; it should be made an hour or two before dinner that the flavor may be well extracted; is considered almost indispensible with roast lamb.

513. Oyster Sauce—From half a pint of oysters carefully remove all bits of shell, and set over the fire in a pint of boiling water and let it boil three minutes; skim well and stir in a half cup butter, beaten to a cream, with two tablespoons flour; let it come to a boil. Is served with boiled turkey.

514. Oyster Sauce—Make a white sauce, No. 515; boil the oysters slightly, and mix thoroughly with the same.

515. White Sauce—Put two ounces of butter in a small sauce-pan, set it on the fire, stir a little, and as soon as melted remove to a slower fire; add a tablespoon of flour, stir continually till thoroughly mixed, and gently pour in a pint of boiling water, stirring continually; when it begins to thicken take off the fire; add the yelk of an egg, beaten with a teaspoon of cold water; mix it well with the sauce; season with salt and pepper, and it is done.

516. Orange Hard Sauce—Select a thin-skinned orange, carefully peel it in six even parts towards the stem end, preserving it whole; extract the juice and mix it with a light, moist (extra C) sugar sufficient to form into a ball nearly the size of the orange originally, which place in the peel and serve. A lemon sauce may be prepared the same way.

517. A Sweet Sauce for Puddings—In half a pint of melted butter with milk stir three tablespoons powdered or granulated sugar, a little grated lemon-rind, nutmeg or powdered cinnamon; other flavoring fancied may be added to the milk in preparing the butter; is served with rice, batter or bread puddings.

518. Sour Sauce—Mix one and a-half cups sugar and half a tablespoon flour in a little water; add two tablespoons vinegar or lemon juice, a quarter of a nutmeg grated and a pinch of salt; pour over it one and a-half pints boiling water, and boil ten minutes; just before taking up add a tablespoon of butter.

519. A Sauce for Fritters—See under Fritters No. 90.

CATSUPS.

Note.—In making any kind of catsup use a granite or porcelain kettle; never in mettle, or it will not only discolor but affect its flavor. Always select perfect fruit, vegetables or other materials, and keep in stone or glass bottles or jars; never use tin cans with any expectation that it will not spoil, or preserve its original taste. It will be less apt to mould if the bottles or jars are not filled quite to the top. Some fill up with hot vinegar. Should there be a skim of mould over the top when opened, remove every particle and the catsup will be uninjured. When, however, there appears white specks through it, it is irretrievably spoiled.

After opening, if too thick, add vinegar sufficient to thin; or, if in danger of souring before it is all used, scalding will prevent it.

520. Mushroom Catsup—Use the larger kind, known as umbrella or "flaps." They must be very fresh and not gathered in very wet weather, or the catsup will be less apt to keep. Wash and cut them in two to four pieces, and place them in a wide flat jar or crock in layers, sprinkling each layer with salt, and let them stand for twenty-four hours; take them out and press out the juice, when bottle and cork; put the mushrooms back again, and in another twenty-four hours press them again, bottle and cork; repeat this for the third time, and then mix together all the juice extracted; add to it pepper, allspice, one or more cloves, according to quantity, pounded together; boil the whole, and skim as long as any scum rises; bottle when cool; put in each bottle two cloves and a pepper-corn. Cork and seal, put in a dry place, and it will keep for years.

521. Tomato Catsup—Take one bushel of solid ripe tomatoes; clean them with a wet cloth, cut off any unripe part about the stem end, or any warts or blemish; put them in a granite or porcelain-lined kettle, or a genuine bell-metal one, never let them come in contact with iron; pour over them about three pints of water; add ten or twelve onions or shallots, cut fine; boil until soft; some take about two hours; strain through a coarse sieve, pour the liquid back again into the boiling kettle, and add half a gallon of good cider vinegar; then take two ounces ground spice, two ounces ground black pepper, two ounces mustard (seed or ground, as preferred), one ounce ground cloves, two grated nutmegs, two pounds light brown sugar, and one pint of salt; mix these ingredients well together and put in the boiler, boiling two hours, stirring continually to prevent burning; cayenne pepper to be added to taste if wished hot. When cool, fill bottles or jars. Cork and seal with wax, so as to exclude the air (see note for directions regarding preservation of catsup). Keep in a cool, dry place.

PICKLES.

Note—For pickles use the best cider or white wine vinegar, when the latter can be procured, and not an acid vinegar, so called. It can not be too strong, as it is weakened when scalded to pour over the pickles. Unscalded vinegar does not keep well with pickles.

Never use a metal vessel in pickling; it should be either the new granite ware or porcelain, and keep in stone or glass, in the cellar or other cool, dark place. They should be examined frequently, and soft ones removed; if white specks appear in the vinegar drain it off and scald, add a half tea-cup of sugar to each gallon and pour again over the pickles; a few bits of horse-radish or a few cloves in the vinegar will aid in maintaining its life.

All vegetables or fruit for pickling, except for sweet pickles, should be sound, but not quite ripe. Do not scald cucumbers, but soak them in salt and water. Boiled beets can be pickled whole, first removing the skin, to be sliced when required. Vegetables that require to be boiled or scalded before pickling will be whiter if a little lemon or green grape juice is added to the water, as cabbage, cauliflower, melons, mangoes, white beets or onions. Care should be used not to scald too much, or they will be soft and tasteless. For green vegetables put a little soda in the water to preserve the color. Always have the vegetables or fruit perfectly cold before pouring over the vinegar, which should be in all cases very hot.

A good average of spices to a quart of pickles is an even teaspoon of each of allspice, pepper corns, half each of mustard seed or horse-radish finely chopped, a tablespoon of stick cinnamon broken, and a piece of Jamaica ginger an inch long.

522. Pickled Cucumbers—The small green ones, termed gherkins, are the best to use. Clean them well in cold water with a brush, removing all prickles, and soak in a strong rock-salt brine for about three days; take them out and put into wide-mouthed bottles or jars, with a few cloves of garlic, pepper-corns, cloves, rock-salt, and a bunch of seasonings, composed of bay leaves, tarragon, or other flavoring herbs, to taste, all tied in a Swiss muslin bag; fill each jar with vinegar as soon as it boils, and when they are perfectly cold cover them air-tight. They should be looked at every two or three days for first three weeks, and should the pickles or vinegar turn white, throw away the vinegar and spices, and add new hot vinegar and fresh spices; cover when cold as before. Small white onions may be pickled with the cucumbers if desired.

523. Pickled Onions—Select small silver-skinned onions; remove with a knife all the outer skins, so that each onion will be perfectly white and clean; soak them in strong brine three days, drain. Place in a jar first a layer of onions three inches deep, then sprinkle with a mixture of the following: Two teaspoons each chopped horse-radish and cloves, four tablespoons cinnamon bark and half a teaspoon cayenne pepper to each gallon of pickles; then another layer of onions, and repeat until jar is filled; bring vinegar to boiling point; add brown sugar in the proportion of a quart to a gallon, and pour hot over the onions.

524. Piccalilli—One large white cabbage, fifty small cucumbers (gherkins), five quarts small string beans, eight small carrots, one dozen sticks celery, five red peppers, three green peppers, two heads cauliflower; chop fine, soak over night in salt and water; wash well, drain thoroughly, and pour over them hot vinegar spiced with mace, cinnamon and allspice; turn off vinegar and scald; place in common well covered jars, or seal in cans while hot.

525. Sweet Pickles—They may be made of any fruit that can be preserved, including the rinds of ripe watermelons and cucumbers. The syrup is made in the proportions of three pints of sugar to a quart of vinegar. Use the best vinegar and "C" coffee or best brown sugar. The spices to be used are principally stick cinnamon and whole cloves; the latter stuck in the fruit if desired highly spiced.

526. Sweet Pickle for Fruit—For each seven pounds of fruit take four pounds light brown sugar, one pint vinegar, half an ounce cloves and the same of cinnamon; boil all but the fruit two mornings in succession, and pour over the fruit; the third morning boil all together.

H. WICHERT,

77, 79, 81 & 83 W. Lake Street,

CHICAGO

MANUFACTURER

MUSTARD

AND

PICKLES

Olive & Salad Oils.

PREPARER OF

HORSE RADISH,

Genuine Tomato Catsup

AND

Table Sauces.

JELLIES AND PRESERVES.

Note—Of the different sweetmeats compounded with sugar are jellies, preserves, marmalades, jams and candied fruits.

In producing any of the above the greatest care must be taken, as economy of time will be likely to prove a waste of material. All fruits employed should be of the freshest, and if possible those gathered in the morning, in dry weather, when they will possess the fullest flavor and keep longer.

The best sugar is the most economical for preserves, jams, etc., and clarified or loaf sugar for jellies. For clear, transparent syrups used in preserves, refined sugars must be used, although darker shades may be clarified.

The utensils used should be of porcelain, granite-ware, block-tin, genuine bell metal, copper or brass. The three last should be kept particularly bright and clean. It is better to use a boxwood or wedgewood-ware spoon, rather than metal, for all purposes of stirring or handling.

JELLIES.

Note—Fruit jellies are compounded of the juice of fruits, combined with sugar, concentrated by boiling to such a consistency that the liquid upon cooling assumes the form of a tremulous jelly. Many fruits do not contain sufficient gelatine properties to assume the jelly form, when the refined gelatine or isinglass must be used in sufficient quantities to produce that result. The best meat jellies are made from calves' feet or head, by the addition of sugar and flavors.

A jelly bag is an essential to jelly making, and is made as follows: Use a stout white flannel cloth (that called double-milled, much used for ironing blankets, is the best); cut it in the shape of a fool's cap, lap the edges, and stitch each edge. The most convenient way of using is to tie it on a hoop the exact size of the mouth of the bag, for which purpose several tapes should be sewn round the edge at equal distances. A convenient way of using is to suspend it from the back of a chair. Jellies are moulded in various fanciful forms, the moulds for which are formed of tinned copper or block-tin, and may be procured at any housekeeping emporium. The jellies may be moulded at any time before using, after having been bottled or kept in jars, by simply melting and pouring into the moulds previously soaked in cold water. To remove from the mould set them in hot water for a moment. Additional flavors may be added at this time.

Jellies should be kept in glass jars or tumblers, and may be filled with the boiling liquid without cracking them, if previously greased on the outside with a little butter or lard and pouring in the first spoon or two slowly. Cover with writing paper cut to fit, pressed closely over the jelly, and put on the lid or cover with thick paper, rubbed over on the inside with the white of an egg.

Jelly needs more attention in damp or rainy weather than in other. It should be examined occasionally, and if there are any signs of fermentation reboil and strain.

527. Calves Foot Stock for Jellies—It should be made at least one day before it is required for use, so it may be well cooled, and all fat can then be more thoroughly removed. Procure two nicely-dressed calves feet, wash them, remove the fat from between the toes, and put into six pints cold water, which gradually bring to a boil, removing all scum as it rises. Boil it gently six to seven hours, until the water is reduced about half, then strain it through a sieve into a basin, and place in a cool place to set. When straining, measure the liquor. To clarify it remove all fat from the top, and pour over a little warm water to remove any remaining, and wipe the jelly with a clean cloth. Remove the jelly from all sediment, and put it in a sauce-pan; add to it six ounces loaf sugar (to the quart), the shells and well-beaten whites of five eggs, stirring all together cold; set all on the fire, and do not stir it after it commences to warm; ten minutes after it rises to a head, and kept boiling, throw in a cup cold water, let it boil five minutes longer and take it off the fire; closely cover the sauce-pan and let it stand half an hour near the fire; wring the jelly-bag out in hot water quite dry, hang it on the back of a chair near the fire, place a bowl underneath to catch the jelly, and pour it into the bag; should it not be clear the first time run it through again. This stock is the base for all good meat jellies, and by the addition of wine, liquors and coloring, or by moulding with fresh or preserved fruits, a great variety of jellies may be produced. Larger quantities produced by using larger proportions. Two calves' feet should make a quart of stock. To insure its jellying sufficiently hard, a half ounce of isinglass or gelatine can be added.

528. Fruit Jellies—To extract the juice place the fruit in a kettle with just enough water to keep from burning, stir often and let it remain on the fire until sufficiently scalded; or, perhaps a better but slower method is to place it in a stone jar, set in a kettle of warm water and boil until the fruit is well moistened, stirring often and then strain through the jelly-bag, emptying and thoroughly rinsing it each time it is used. Two or three pints of jelly is all that should be made at once, as larger quantities require much longer boiling. The rule is to use equal quantities of juice and sugar. Boil the juice rapidly ten minutes from the first moment of boiling, add the sugar and boil ten minutes longer. The larger fruits, as apples and quinces, should be cut in pieces, the cores and all defects removed; water added to just cover and boiled gently until tender. Jelly may be tested by dropping into a glass of cold water; if it at once sinks to the bottom it is done.

PRESERVES.

Note—Preserves are any kind of fruit or vegetables which it is desirable or may be kept by means of drying or in a syrup, formed wholly or in part with sugar, according to the nature of the material to be preserved. Keep all fruits to be preserved in an ice-house or refrigerator until required, and they will remain plump and fresh several days. Fruit gathered in wet or foggy weather will be nearly worthless for preserving. Preserves should be only gently boiled to avoid danger of burning. For clear or transparent syrups, refined sugar should be used, although the darker shades may be clarified. The longer it is boiled the thicker will be its consistency. A solution of two parts of sugar to one of water, and boiling but little, will afford a syrup of the right strength to neither ferment or crystallize; another in the proportion of half a pint of water to a pound of sugar is also used for most fruits.

Formerly it was considered that an equal weight of sugar was required to preserve fruit; but, since the introduction of hermetically sealed jars or cans, a half to three-quarters of a pound is deemed sufficient when so put up.

Fruits, except as mentioned, require to be prepared by boiling until sufficiently tender for the syrup to penetrate. Some fruits, as apples, peaches, tomatoes, plums, strawberries, that are likely to become too soft by previous boiling, may have the sugar strewn over them and allowed to stand a few hours, when they are scalded and canned or put in jars. Another method to also retain the original hardness of the fruit, is to take it out of the syrup after boiling a few minutes and place it in the sun for two or three hours, and then pour over it the boiling syrup. Other fruits, as pears, citrons or quinces, harden when put into a thick syrup equal to their weight in sugar, to obviate which they may be cooked until tender in a weaker syrup, made with only a portion of the sugar and the remainder afterwards added. Jams and marmalades are of the same nature as preserves, differing but little from each other, being preserves of a half liquid consistency made by boiling the pulp of the fruit with sugar. Jams are made from the more juicy berries and currants, as blackberries, raspberries and mulberries. Marmalades are compounded with the firmer fruits — pineapples, peaches, quinces and the rinds of oranges.

Preserves may be packed for keeping in tin, glass or earthenware, cans, bottles or jars. It is a good plan to fill a small can or jar for present use, to prevent opening the larger ones too frequently.

529. Clarified Syrup—A clarified syrup is produced by dissolving two pounds of refined sugar, not necessarily white, unless desired for white fruits, in a pint of water; add to it the white of an egg, and beat it well; put it in a preserving-pan on the fire, and stir with a wooden spoon. As soon as it begins to swell and boil up throw in a little cold water or sweet oil to dampen; let it boil up again, take it off, and remove all scum; boil again; throw in more cold water; remove scum, and repeat if necessary. It may be considered sufficiently boiled when it pours off the spoon like oil.

530. Dried Preserves—Any of the fruits that have been preserved in syrup may be converted into dry preserves, by first draining them from the syrup and then drying them slowly on the stove, strewing them thickly with powdered sugar. They should be turned every few hours, sifting over them more sugar.

THE
WESTERN MARKET

680 W. Lake Street,

Three Doors West of Wood,

Is the Place for the Best Quality of

⇢MEATS⇠

Etc., at Reasonable Prices.

C. MACKNESS, PROPRIETOR.

CHOICE

BUTTER & EGGS

A SPECIALTY.

HEISSLER & JUNGE,

345, 347 & 349 State St.; Branch, 433 State St.,

WHOLESALE AND RETAIL

BAKERS & CONFECTIONERS

Ornamented Cakes and Pyramids for Parties and Weddings supplied at the shortest notice.

TEA, COFFEE, CHOCOLATE, ETC.

Tea—*Note*—The botanical name of the shrub or tree is *Camillia Thea*. Neither its origin nor the date of its first cultivation in China is now known. The teas of China are classed as black and green—distinctions not of different species of the plant, but to the age of the leaf, when gathered, and method of preservation. Each has several sub-varieties, named from the district from which produced, or some peculiarity in the article itself. The quality of tea depends greatly upon the age of the leaf at the time of picking, the younger the leaves the more delicate the flavor. Of black teas are Bohea, Congou, Souchong, Caper, Oolong, Pekoe and others, the highest quality of which is Pekoe, and the coarsest, Bohea. When the leaves are so very young as to be covered with a down, it constitutes the Flowery Pekoe. The green teas comprise Twankay, Young Hyson, Old Hyson, Hyson Skin, Imperial and Gunpowder, the latter being the first gathering and the finest. Imperial, Young and Old Hyson are grades from second and third pickings, while the inferior light leaves winnowed from the Hysons form the Hyson Skin. Of the teas of Japan, they are classed according to manner of curing, as basket-fired, pan-fired and sun-dried; are grown in two crops, the spring and fall, the latter being the best. Originally, Japanese teas were uncolored, but now they have quite as much coloring added as those of China, while they lack the body of the latter.

Teas are subject to various adulterations, both in China and the countries where sold, including the mixing of different qualities, coloring, and other treatment, to improve the appearance of different kinds.

The most important constituent of tea is *theine*, identical with *caffeine*, the active principal of coffee. Genuine teas have also 20 to 40 per cent. of tannic acid, which gives the tea its astringency, but the aroma and a large share of the flavor is dependent upon the amount of aromatic oil and theine to be extracted. When tea is infused too long the tannic acid is developed, and is denoted by marked astringency. In England and America sugar and milk or cream, one or both, are generally added, but by many it is thought to detract from the flavor of fine teas, rather than to be a desirable addition.

531. *Tea Dust*, now generally kept on sale by grocers and tea dealers, is the siftings of finer grades of tea carefully saved and imported. While afforded at a much less price than regular tea, it is much stronger and usually superior to cheap grades of tea. The chief objection to its use is its pulverized condition. This may be obviated, however, by the use of a wire tea-ball, or a bag suspended in the pot similar to that suggested for coffee; or it may be poured through a fine strainer to the cups. Much less is required for the production of good tea than the regular leaf.

532. *Tea Making*—Is not a difficult process, a few simple directions being observed. The hotter tea is served the better, and is worthless and insipid when but warm. A teaspoon of the leaf to each person and one over is the rule in using teas of ordinary quality, and it may here be observed that the better grades, and consequent higher priced teas, possessing the greater amount of the constituents of good tea, are really the most economical to use. The pot or urn should be well warmed with hot water, letting it stand two or three minutes, and then either used to also warm the cups or discharged. Put in the tea, and add a half to three-quarters pint of boiling water; let it stand to draw, but not boil, from five to ten minutes (some consider a medium of seven minutes about right), and then fill up with boiling water. When there is a large party to provide for, it is better to have two tea-pots, instead of having a large quantity in one. The infusion being once completed, the addition of fresh tea will add very little to its strength, so it is much better to commence anew when more is required. The character of the water also influences the quality of the tea, it being impossible to make really good tea with hard water. Excess of lime in the water may be corrected by the use of a little carbonate of soda, and some think it assists in extracting the better qualities of the tea. For mixed teas, the proportion used is generally four teaspoons of black to one of green; more of the latter when that flavor is desired to predominate. The remarks concerning the coffee-pot or urn will equally apply to the tea-pot.

533. Iced Teas—Are now served to considerable extent during the summer months. They are of course used without milk, and the addition of sugar serves only to destroy the finer tea flavor. It may be prepared some hours in advance, and should be made stronger than when served hot. It is bottled and placed in the ice-chest till required. Use the black or green teas, or both, mixed, as fancied.

534. Coffee—*Note*—The cultivation of this esteemed berry is widely diffused throughout the tropical belt nearly around the world. Its name is said to be derived from *Kaffa*, a district lying south of Abyssinia, where it was first cultivated and used as a beverage. In most countries it is picked by hand; but in Arabia it is left to ripen until nearly ready to fall. This may be one reason for its strong and superior flavor. The active principle of coffee is caffeine, and is employed to some extent in medicine. Coffee possesses considerable nourishing qualities, and both tea and coffee produce an agreeable, exhilarating effect, being a stimulant without being an intoxicant. When taken in quantities or quite strong, it produces wakefulness and is not beneficial to the system. The popular taste, like that for tea, is very extended, those of strong flavor being most in demand.

Of the different coffees imported here, Java and Mocha rank the highest with connoisseurs, and are generally used mixed in the proportion of four to six ounces of Mocha to the pound. The bulk of all coffee used in this country is Rio, Santos, or those of South or Central American production. The former possesses a strong but not delicate flavor, while the latter are milder. The West India islands produce fine coffees, which are known under their respective names, as San Salvador, Costa Rica, La Guara, etc.

535. Ground Coffee—As it is rather generally believed that all put up or ground coffees sold in bulk are more or less adulterated with peas, carrots, chiccory or more harmful substances, the safest way is to either purchase the green berry and brown it yourself, or freshly browned and ground at the time it is bought; a small quantity frequently, that it may not lose the flavor before consumed. Some persons like the flavor of chiccory, and it may be purchased of itself and mixed with good coffee in the proportion of a teaspoon to each quarter of a pound. A good substitute is also browned and ground carrot, using two teaspoons to same quantity of coffee as above.

To test the genuineness of ground coffee, take a pinch between the wetted finger and thumb, roll it, and if pure it will remain in grains; if adulterated it will form into a ball.

When freshly browned coffee may not be obtained, the following French method is probably the best for roasting, as it is said to develop the strength and flavor more thoroughly.

536. *To Roast Coffee*—Pick over, wash, and dry enough for a week only, and to each three pounds add a lump of good butter, the size of a large hickory nut, when the coffee is hot; roast in a revolving roaster, which, if constantly turned, will roast more evenly than by stirring in a dripping-pan. If no regular roaster is convenient, brown it in the oven, or on the top of the stove or range, watching and stirring continually, that it may not burn; a single berry when burned will taint the whole mass, and the flavor, which is very volatile, pervade the whole house. It should be roasted evenly a dark rich brown, and should be tested frequently, by placing a kernel on the table, pressing it with the thumb, and if tender and brittle, so it crushes easily, it is done. When roasted properly it will grind into particles, distinct and granulated. Coffee swells about one-third in bulk, and loses about sixteen per cent. in roasting. When roasted, keep in an air-tight tin can or box, and grind only medium fine the quantity needed, immediately before using.

537. *To Make Coffee*—To extract and retain the greatest amount of aroma is the great object to be attained in coffee making, and to effect this in the most effectual manner opinions differ. Many consider that percolation, filtering, or leeching is the best process, and to this end there are many contrivances, both in this country and in England and France, among which may be mentioned the French biggin, the English syphon iron, the National or old Dominion coffee-pot, the coffee and tea-press, and many others, all of which filter or leech hot water through ground coffee, and most of them produce a clear, rich fluid, probably as near perfect as possible. The theory is that by boiling, the finest and greater part of the aroma escapes in the vapor.

To the filtering process many object on economical grounds, urging that not more than half the virtue of the coffee is extracted, and hence it takes very much more than by slightly boiling. The following method partakes of both, and also obviates the purchase of an expensive utensil.

Take an ordinary coffee-pot, the spout having a tight-fitting cover; form a ring of thick wire that will fit just outside the top of the pot, leaving a space for the hinge, if any ; to this attach a thin but stout muslin bag, wider at the bottom than top, and reaching to within two inches of the bottom; the seams should be lapped and doubly-stitched, that none of the ground coffee may escape into the pot; warm the pot thoroughly with boiling water and empty; place the bag containing the quantity of ground coffee required, and pour over it gradually boiling water; when it has filtered through it may then be served, or brought to a boil first, as desired; remove the bag before sending to table, using the same pot. The quantity of coffee to use depends much on the kind or quality, but a heaping table-spoon, or half an ounce, is usually sufficient for each person, with one over if there are several.

Coffees that are not made in either of the above methods, but the coffee put directly into the pot, boil rather fast for three to five minutes, and then set back on the stove for ten or fifteen minutes longer. Coffee may be cleared or settled by the addition of part of the white of an egg, egg-shells, or cod-fish skin, mixed with or put in at same time as the coffee; or a dash of cold water and letting it stand a minute after, will also clear it. Good cream, instead of milk, will make even an inferior coffee quite drinkable. Milk should always be served hot, and an egg beaten in it just before serving will add greatly to its richness. It should be previously mixed with a few spoons cold milk. Coffee without either milk or cream is said to be the most wholesome, especially for persons of weak digestion. Both coffee and tea pots or urns should be kept excessively clean, and once a week boil a little borax in them, with enough water to cover the whole inside. Never wash them inside. It is quite sufficient to rinse them in two or three waters, and as soon after being used as possible it should be done.

538. Cafe Noir or Black Coffee—Is an after-dinner beverage, generally believed to promote digestion; it is made very strong, using nearly double the usual quantity of coffee, and is served in tiny cups fifteen or twenty minutes after dinner. Gentlemen frequently add a small quantiy of brandy or wine. It may be made by either of the above processes, but filtering is doubtless the best, as it more readily produces a very clear liquid.

539. Chocolate and Cocoa—Are similar preparations from the beans, seeds or nibs of the cacoa, a species of the palm differing from the cocoa-nut tree, and producing large seed-bearing pods; these are roasted similar to coffee, and formed into a paste with (or without) sugar and some other ingredients, and sometimes flavored with a small portion of the vanilla bean. The plain, sweetened, or flavored may be procured in cakes or pulverized. Some of those now manufactured in this country are said to be equal, if not superior, to the French chocolate, long considered unrivalled. The shells or husks winnowed from the beans, called cocoa-shells, make a weaker beverage, sold principally for invalids or persons of poor digestion. Chocolate, when well made, forms a nutritive and salutary beverage.

540. Broma—Is a similar preparation from the cocoa-nut, and sold in packages ready ground. Its use is confined chiefly to invalids and children, to whom the oil in chocolate or cocoa is either not beneficial or distasteful.

Proper directions for use usually accompany either of the above preparations.

THE CENTENNIAL AMERICAN
TEA CO.
DEALERS IN FINE
Teas, Coffees, Sugars AND Spices,
678 W. LAKE STREET.

Principal Warehouse and Coffee Roasting Establishment: 49 Vesey St., New York.

✢ ALLARD ✣

81 Madison Street, Chicago.

ALLARD IS

THE HATTER

At the above number and a resident of Chicago, pursuing the same business for many years. He is the proprietor of the celebrated hat known as the "DRALLARD," and which has extended reputation for style, material and best workmanship.

ALLARD is not a Cheap John. He sells the best of goods, and if his hats fail to give satisfaction from fault of material or manufacture, he replaces them free of charge.

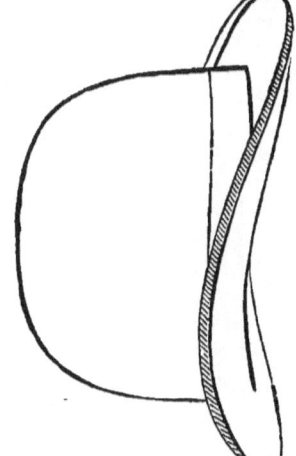

ALLARD

Caters to the trade which demands first-class goods. If that is your style, he respectfully

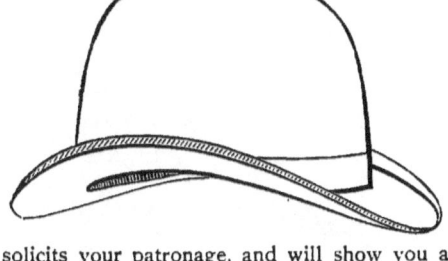

solicits your patronage, and will show you a fine line of

Hats, Caps & Furs
IN THEIR SEASON.

THE LIGHT-RUNNING

NEW HOME

Sewing Machine
is for Sale by Dealers everywhere.

ASK YOUR FRIENDS THAT ALREADY HAVE ONE, WHAT THEY THINK OF IT.

In use in over 560,000 Families!

It has the most handsome appearance and the most perfect attachments. Every Machine warranted for 5 years.

NEW HOME SEWING MACHINE CO.,
248 State Street, Chicago.

INDEX.

No.		Page.	No.		Page.	No.		Page.
	INTRODUCTION	5-6	85	Rice	21	138	Harricot of	34
	BREAD.		88	Pancakes, French	21	139	And Rice	34
			86	Hotel Wellington	21	140	And Tomato Sauce	34
11	Boston Brown	11	87	Indian	21	141	Pie with Tomatoes	34
12	Boston Brown	11		**BATTER AND FRIED CAKES.**		143	Scrambled Mutton	34
95	Brown, Palmer House	22				142	Shepherd's Pie	34
13	Corn, St. Charles Hotel	11	89	Doughnuts	22	144	Mutton and Potato Pie	34
14	Corn	11	90	Fritters, Thomaston	22		**LAMB.**	
15	Corn	11	93	A Sauce for	22			
16	Corn, Steamed	11	92	Apple	22		Note	34
17	Corn, Boston	11	93	Apple	22	150	A la Matelot	35
8	To Cool	10	94	Cream	22	147	Broiled Breast of	35
18	Graham	11	91	Queen	22	148	Chops, Broiled	35
19	Graham and Indian	12	71	Waffles	19	149	Scallop	35
9	Hop Yeast, Bread	10	70	Baking Powder	19	146	Stewed with Peas	35
20	Rye	12	72	Another	19	145	With Mint Sauce	35
21	Rye	12	76	Massasoit House	20		**PORK.**	
19	Rye and Indian	12	74	Raised	20		Note	37
22	Salt Raised	12	75	Rice	20	155	Pork Chops	38
23	Sponge, for Winter	12	73	Quick	20	157	Pork, Fried, Salt	38
10	Twice Raised	10		**FARINACEOUS DISHES.**		158	Fried, Salt	38
7	Yeast Cake	10				159	Grilled, Salt	38
6	Hop	10	68	Cracked Wheat	19	160	And Beans, Yankee	38
3	Potato, from Stock	9	69	Grits or Hominy	19	154	Steaks, Fried	38
4	Potato, with Hops	9	64	Mush, Cornmeal	18	151	Stuffed and Roasted	37
5	Potato, without Hops	9	65	Graham	18	152	Roast Spare-rib	37
1	Stock	9	66	Oatmeal	18	153	Roast Sucking Pig	37
2	Stock	9	67	Oatmeal, Steamed	19	156	Tenderloin	38
	BREAKFAST AND TEA CAKES.			**BEEF.**			**HAM.**	
	Note—Baking Powder, etc.	13		Note, to select, general directions to cook, etc	25		Note	39
35	Biscuit	14	99	Beef, a la Mode	26	161	Ham, Boiled	39
36	Biscuit	14	129	Cakes	31	162	Broiled	39
9	Hop Yeast	10	104	Corned	27	163	Broiled	39
39	Soda	14	103	Boiled	26	164	And Eggs, Fried	39
40	South Carolina	15	105	Pressed	27		**VEAL.**	
37	Hard, Sugar	14	114	Hash	29		Note, to select, etc	41
38	Soft, Sugar	14	127	Cortland	30	174	Veal, Cold, with Tomatoes	42
49	Buns	16	113	Croquettes of	28			
50	Buns	16	107	En Ragout	27	168	Cutlets, fried	42
51	Buns, London Hot Cross	16	109	Fricassee of Cold Roast	26	166	Gravy for Roast	41
34	Cake, Cinnamon	14				175	Patties	43
61	Crackers, Egg	18	111	Pie	28	167	Pie	41
60	Crackers, French	18	112	And Potatoe Pie	28	171	Pot-pie	42
48	Crackuells	16	124	Potted	30	170	Ragout of	42
59	Corn Dodgers	17	98	Ragout of	26	165	Roast Loin of	41
47	Crumpets, English	16	96	Roast	25	169	Stew	42
24	Gems, Graham	13	108	Tomato Sauce	28	173	Toast	42
25	Graham	13	130	Round of	31	172	With Oysters	42
28	Indian	13	202	(A Stuffing for	49	176	Sweetbreads, to select and prepare	43
27	Sweet Milk	13	97	With Pudding	25			
26	Wheaten	13	110	Stewed	28	177	Broiled	43
55	Johnny Cake	17	126	Stewed, Chipped	30	178	Fried	43
56	Johnny Cake	17	106	Spiced Beef Relish	27	179	Fricasseed	43
58	Alabama	17	100	Beefsteak, Broiled	26	180	With Green Peas	43
57	New England	16	101	Fried	26		**POULTRY AND GAME.**	
31	Muffins, Corn	13	102	And Onions	26			
30	Graham	13	125	Staffordshire	30		**POULTRY.**	
29	Wheat	13	128	Filet, Chateaubriand	31	181	Chicken, Baked	45
33	Popovers	14	131	Hamburger Steak	31	182	Baked, with parsnips	45
32	Puffet	14	132	Hamburg Steak	31	183	Boiled	45
43	Rolls, Coffee	15	115	Beef-tongue Hash	29	184	Broiled	45
44	Egg	15	116	Boiled	29	185	Fried, Spring	45
45	Long Breakfast	15	117	Spiced	29	186	Fricasseed	46
41	Parker House	15	118	Calves Liver, Broiled	29	187	Fricasseed	46
42	Vienna	15	119	Calves or Beef Liver, Fried	29	188	Lunch for Traveling	46
52	Rusk	17				189	Pie	46
53	Rusk	17	123	Chipolata	30	191	Pot-pie	46
54	Lebanon	17	120	Tripe, Fried	30	191	Puree of	46
46	Sally Lunn	16	121	Fried in Batter	30	192	Salmi of	47
62	Toast, Economical	18	122	Fricasseed	30	193	Oyster Croquettes	47
63	Excellent	18		**MUTTON AND LAMB.**		194	Salad	47
	GRIDDLE OR BATTER CAKES.			Note, to select, to keep, to cook	33	202	A Stuffing for	49
82	Batter	21				195	Turkey, Roast, Oyster Stuffing	47
79	Bread	20		**MUTTON.**				
77	Buckwheat	20				196	Roast, English style	48
78	Same, without Yeast	20	133	Boiled, Caper Sauce	33	197	Boned	48
81	Corn	20	134	Leg a la Venison	33	198	Boiled, Oyster Stuffing	48
83	Flannel	20	135	Chops, Broiled	33			
84	Graham	21	136	Fried	34	205	Deviled	49
80	Huckleberry	20	137	Fried	34	199	Goose, Roast	49

No.		Page	No.		Page	No.		Page
200	Goose, Deviled	49	291	Oyster Croquettes	65	333	Cabbage, to Select, etc.	74
212	Duck, Roast	51	294	Oysters, Deviled	65	333	To Boil	74
202	A Stuffing for	49	288	Escalloped	65	334	Heidelberg	74
203	Boiled	49	278	Fried	63	335	South Carolina	74
204	Pie	49	280	Fried	63	336	Stuffed	75
			281	Fried	63	337	Carrots, to Prepare	75
	GAME.		279	Boston Fry	63	338	To Boil	75
	Note—Rule for Cooking, etc.	49	290	Oyster Fritters	65	339	Stewed	75
	Note—A Hint to Sportsmen	53	266	Grilled, with Pork	62	340	Cauliflower, to Select,	
210	Duck, Wild, To Select,		269	Panned	62		Clean, Boil, etc.	75
	etc	50	270	Panned	62	341	Corn, Green	75
212	Roast, Tame or Wild	51	292	Patties	65	342	Boiled	75
213	Game Pie	51	293	Patties	65	343	Stewed	75
209	Goose, Roast Wild	50	284	Pie	64	344	Oysters	76
214	Prairie Chicken or		285	Pie	64	345	Fritters or Mock Oys-	
	Pheasant, Roasted	51	286	Pie	64		ters	76
215	Same, Broiled	51	287	Pie	64	346	Cucumbers, Raw	76
226	Pigeons	53	260	Raw, on Half Shell	61	347	Boiled and Fried	76
227	Pot-pie	53	261	Raw, without Shell	61	348	Egg Plant, Fried	76
228	Compote of	53	257	Oysters, Roast in Shell	60	349	Breaded and Fried	76
229	Plover, Broiled	53	258	Fulton Market Roast	61	350	Greens, To Prepare, to	
216	Quail, Roast	52	267	Steamed, Shell	62		Cook	77
184	Broiled	45	268	Steamed, Count	62	351	Mushrooms, Varieties,	
217	On Toast	52	271	Stew	62		to Cook	77
224	Rabbit	53	272	Stew	62	352	Okra	77
225	Roasted	53	276	Boston Fancy	63	353	Onions, Varieties	77
218	Reed Birds, Roast	52	275	Dry Stew	63	355	Baked	78
219	Au Pomme de Terre	52	274	Stew, in Milk or		357	Beefsteak and	78
220	Snipe	52		Cream	63	354	Boiled	77
223	Squirrel, to Prepare and		277	Stew, Neptune	63	356	Fried	78
	Cook	53	273	Stew, Plain	62	358	Oyster Plant	78
215	Broiled	51	289	With Veal	65	359	Parsnips, boiled	78
221	Woodcock, to Broil	52		Note—Clams, varieties, etc.	65	361	Fried	78
221	To Roast	52	295	Clam Chowder — New		360	Stewed	78
222	Fried	52		Bedford recipe	66	362	Peas, Green	78
206	Venison, to Choose	50	296	Clam Chowder	66	363	In Cream	78
206	To Keep	50	299	Fried	66	364	Dry or Split	79
206	To Cook	50	300	Fried, Breaded	66		Note—Potatoes, brief histo-	
207	Roast Saddle	50	302	Fritters—Hotel Wel-			ry, to Select, to Keep.	79
208	Roast Haunch	50		lington	67		To Cook, etc	80
			303	Fritters	67	366	A la Francaise	80
	FISH.		301	Pie	67	365	A la Parisienne	80
			297	Stew	66	375	Balls	82
	Note—Fish, To Select, etc.	55	298	And Oyster Stew	66	372	Fried raw	81
230	Fish, Boiled or Steamed			Note—Lobsters	67	373	Fried boiled	81
	General Directions	55	304	Lobsters, Boiled	67	368	Kentucky style	81
231	Steamed	56	306	Croquettes	68	367	Lyonnaise	81
232	Codfish, Boiled, Fresh	56	307	Deviled	68	374	Mashed	81
233	Boiled, Fresh	56	308	Scalloped	68	374	Another Method	81
234	Broiled, Fresh	56	305	Steamed	68	371	Ringed	81
235	Salt, a la Mode	56	309	Crabs	68	369	Saratoga Chips	81
236	Salt, Stewed	56	310	Soft Shell	68	376	Snow	82
237	Picked	56	311	Long Island Style	69	370	Tremont	81
238	Minced Fresh	57	312	Deviled	69	377	For each day of the	
239	Cod, Au Fromage	57	313	Shrimps	69		week	82
240	Codfish Balls	57	314	Terrapin, Maryland		383	Pumpkin	83
241	Salmon, Trout or Pick-			Style	69	378	Sweet Potatoes, Origin,	
	erel, Baked	57		Note—Frogs	69		Varieties, etc	82
242	White Fish or Shad,		315	Fried	69	378	To Cook	83
	Baked	57	316	Stewed	60	379	To Cook various	
244	Broiled	58					ways	83
243	White Fish, Boiled	58		**VEGETABLES.**		380	Baked	83
245	Salt, Broiled	58				381	Salsify	83
246	Fish, Fried	58		Note—General Directions,		382	Squash, Summer	83
250	Stewed	59		Selection and		383	Winter or Pumpkin	83
249	Pan	59		Cooking	71	383	Hubbard	83
253	Chowder	59	317	Asparagus	71	384	Tomato, Nativity of, Cul-	
247	Brook Trout	58	318	To Cook	72		tivation, to Select	83
255	Haddock, Crumbed	59	319	Another method	72	385	Fresh, to serve Raw	84
256	Halibut, Pickled	60	320	Beans	72	386	Baked	84
251	Mackerel, Boiled, Salt	59	321	Butter or Wax	72	387	Stewed	84
252	Broiled, Salt	59	325	Dry	73	388	Stuffed and baked	84
254	Salmon Gratin	59	325	To Boil	73	389	Turnips	84
248	Smelts, Fried	59	325	With Pork or Bacon	73	390	Dried	84
			323	Green, String, etc	72			
	SHELL FISH.		322	String	72		**EGGS AND MACARONI.**	
	Note—Oysters, Varieties, to		326	Green, Shelled	72		Note — Eggs — Nutriment,	
	Select, to Keep, etc.	60	327	Baked	73		Variety, etc	87
259	Oysters, Baked in Shell	61	328	Beets, to Prepare, to			To Select	87
262	Boiled in Shell	61		Cook, to Pickle	73		To Keep	87
263	Broiled in Shell	61	329	Roasted	74	391	Eggs—Boiled, Time, etc	88
264	Broiled, Count	61	330	Harvest	74	397	Baked	90
265	Broiled	61	331	Stewed	74	392	Omelets	89
282	Broiled	64	332	Broccoli	74	393	Plain Omelet	89
283	Fricasseed	64				394	Another Method	89

No.		Page
395	Eggs, Omelet, Souffle...	90
396	Scrambled	90
398	Macaroni	90
400	Macaroni	90
399	A la Riccadonna	90

SOUPS AND BROTHS.

No.		Page
	Note	93
401	Soup Stock	93
401	Seasonings, Ingredients, General Directions	93–94
404	Bean, cheap and nutritious	95
411	Chicken	96
412	Chicken, with Rice...	96
407	Economical	95
402	English Game	94
410	Gumbo	96
411	Gumbo	96
403	Mock Turtle	95
408	Potato	96
405	Tomato	95
406	Tomato	95
409	Broth—Hulled Corn	96
413	Force Meat Balls for Mock Turtle Soup...	96
402	Force Meat Balls for Game Soups	94

SALADS AND DRESSINGS.

No.		Page
	Note—General Directions...	99

RELISHES.

414	Celery	99
415	Chiccory	99
416	Cress or Water Cress...	99
415	Endive	99
417	Horse Radish	99
418	Lettuce	99
419	Radishes	100
420	Parsley	100
422	Pepper Grass	100
421	Sorrel	100

SALADS.

425	Plain Cold Slaw	100
423	Salad, Bean	100
424	Cabbage	100
426	Chicken	100
427	Chicken	100
428	Chicken	100
194	Chicken, without Celery	47
429	Cucumber	100
430	Lettuce	101
431	Lobster	101
432	Potato (hot)	101
433	Potato (cold)	101

DRESSINGS.

435	Cabbage Salad	101
434	Cream for Cold Slaw	101
436	Mayonaise	101
184	Gravy, Broiled Chicken	45
185	For Fried Chicken	45
181	For Roast Chicken	45
203	For Ducks or Geese	49
196	For Roast Turkey	48
166	For Roast Veal	41
202	Stuffing for Beef, Chickens or Ducks	49
151	For Roast Pork	37
153	For Roast Pig	37
165	For Roast Veal	41

PUDDINGS AND PASTRY.

PUDDINGS.

	Note—General Directions	103
438	Apple Roley Poley	103
440	BlancMange, CornStarch	104
440	A Custard for	104
437	Pudding, Apple	103
443	Cheap and Delicious	104

No.		Page
439	Pudding, Cabinet	104
441	English Plum	104
442	Rice, without Eggs	104
444	Rice, Meringue	104
445	Plain Fruit	105
446	Snow	105
447	Suet	105
448	Sweet	105
97	Yorkshire	25

PASTRY.

	Note—General Directions	105
	The Oven	106
167	Crust for Meat Pies	41
450	Puff Paste	106
452	Pie, Apple Custard	107
454	Cream	107
455	Date	107
457	Lemon	107
456	Another, with Meringue	107
459	Mock Mince	107
460	Pumpkin	107
460	Squash	107
458	Mince Meat	107
451	Patties, Shells for Tarts	106
453	Tarts, Apple	107
453	Meringue for same	107

CAKE AND CONFECTIONERY.

CAKE.

	General Directions and Ingredients	109
	Oven, to Keep	110
461	Cake, Coldwater Pound	110
463	Delicious	110
464	French Chocolate	110
466	Lemon	110
468	Marble	110
471	Spice	111
472	Sponge	111
473	Sponge—More simple	111
474	Cream Frosting for	112
475	Hard or Plain Icing	112
476	Soft Icing for	112
462	Cookies, Cocoanut	110
465	Jumbles	110
467	Lemon Snaps	110
469	Molasses Gingerbread	111
470	Neapolitans	111

CONFECTIONERY.

	Note	112
480	Butter Scotch	113
478	Candies, Various	112
485	Candy, Hoarhound	113
481	Ice Cream	113
486	Molasses	113
479	Rock	113
487	Caramel, or Burnt Sugar	113
482	Chocolate Caramels	113
477	Clarifying Syrup	112
483	Cocoanut Drops	113
484	Hickory-nut Macaroons	113

CUSTARDS, CREAMS AND ICES.

	Note—Custards, general directions for production of all kinds	115
440	Custard, for blancmange	104
488	Ice Creams, varieties	115
489	Materials	115
490	The Cream	115
491	Neapolitan	116
492	Philadelphia	116
493	The Freezer for	116
494	Freezing of	116
495	Water Ices	117
496	General directions for all varieties of	117
497	Molding of	117
498	Granites or Frappes	117

No.		Page
499	Ice, Orange, Lemon, Strawberry, etc	117
500	Pine-apple	117

SAUCES, CATSUPS AND PICKLES.

SAUCES.

	Note—Sauces—General Remarks upon	119
507	Drawn Butter	120
501	Sauce, Anchovy	119
502	Apple	119
503	Caper or Nasturtion	119
504	Chili	119
505	Chili	120
506	Cranberry	120
241	Egg, for Fish	57
242	Fish	57
90	For Fritters	22
508	Green Tomato	120
147	For Breast of Lamb	35
509	Lemon	120
516	Lemon, Hard	121
510	Lobster	120
511	Mayonnaise	120
512	Mint	120
145	Mint	35
513	Oyster	121
514	Oysters	121
515	Orange, Hard	121
517	Sweet, for Puddings	121
518	Sour, for Puddings	121
519	White	121

CATSUPS.

	Note—To Make, to Keep	121
520	Catsup, Mushroom	122
521	Tomato	122

PICKLES.

	Note—General Directions for Pickling	122
522	Pickled Cucumbers	123
523	Onions	123
524	Picalilli	123
525	Pickles, Sweet	123
526	Sweet Pickle for Fruit	123

JELLIES AND PRESERVES.

	General Note on Sweet Compounds	125
	Note—Jellies, Fruits, Jellybag, to Keep, etc	125
527	Jellies — Calves' Foot, Stock for	126
528	Fruit	126
	Note — Preserves—Fruits. Method to Keep	127
	Jams and Marmalades	127
529	Preserves-Clarified Syrup for	127
530	Dried	127

TEA, COFFEE, CHOCOLATE, ETC.

	Note—Tea, General Remarks	129
531	Tea Dust	129
532	Making	129
533	Iced	130
534	Coffee—Note	130
535	Coffee, ground	130
536	To Roast	131
537	To Make by Filtering Process	131
537	Other Methods	131
537	Coffee or Tea Pots, to Cleanse	132
538	CafeNoir or Black Coffee	132
539	Chocolate or Cocoa	132
539	Cocoa Shells	132
540	Broma	132

→THE ONLY←
TOILET SOAP

SUITABLE TO
Remove Stains and Odors from the Hands
—IS—

This Soap contains Pure Sweet Cream so saponified as to retain all the softening and healing properties of

PURE SWEET CREAM.

It will keep the skin soft and white, and prevent roughness where other soaps fail.

G. A. WRISLEY & CO.
MANUFACTURERS,
CHICAGO, ILL.

"The Great Rock Island Route"

MAINTAINS THE LEAD AS THE PEOPLE'S FAVORITE BETWEEN

CHICAGO AND PEORIA, ROCK ISLAND, DAVENPORT, DES MOINES, COUNCIL BLUFFS, OMAHA, LEAVENWORTH, ATCHISON AND KANSAS CITY.

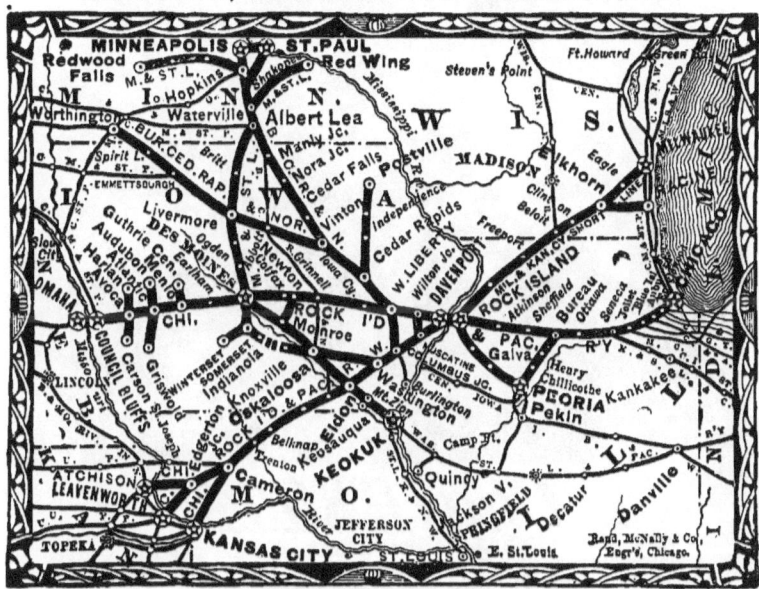

ITS FAMOUS ADJUNCT

"The Albert Lea Route"

Which passes through the most fertile and picturesque region in the central West, is chosen by all who would enjoy the beautiful and travel in ease and comfort, between

CHICAGO, MINNEAPOLIS AND ST. PAUL

No Transfers made between Chicago and the Missouri River or the Upper Mississippi.

Close connections are made in Union Depots with all of the Pacific Railroads, and tickets are sold to all points in

KANSAS, NEBRASKA, COLORADO, NEW MEXICO, ARIZONA, CALIFORNIA, OREGON, WASHINGTON TERRITORY, BRITISH COLUMBIA, NEVADA, UTAH, IDAHO, MONTANA, WYOMING, DAKOTA AND MANITOBA.

2 THROUGH EXPRESS TRAINS EACH WAY DAILY.

Parlor Chair Cars. Pullman Palace Sleeping Cars. World Famous Dining Cars.

R. R. CABLE, Pres't & Gen'l Manager,   E. ST. JOHN, Gen'l Tk't & Pass. Agt.

Chas H. Slack
··· THE ···
GROCER
79 & 81 State Street, Chicago, Ill.

TO HOUSEKEEPERS.

The economical, thrifty and close buyers will make no mistake in perusing our Catalogue and PRICE-CURRENT, and more particularly notice brands and prices as enumerated. There are no two jobbing houses in the city that carry as large varieties of Staple and Fancy **Groceries, Green and Dried Fruits, Flour, Wines, Liquors, Cigars**, etc., and make as many cash sales each day. All goods in original packages are sold as close as any jobber offers the same BRANDS.

Our trade extends over Western Pennsylvania, Ohio, Indiana, Illinois, Wisconsin, Michigan, Minnesota, Iowa, Missouri, Texas, Kansas, Nebraska, the Territories, and all Post-Trader Depots.

N.B.—A complete catalogue sent on application.

View of Niagara Falls from Suspension Bridge.

Starucca Valley, on the Erie.

THE

Scenic Route

OF

→ AMERICA ←

A continual Panorama of Magnificent Scenery from the Lakes to the Seaboard. The Elegant Pullman Service via the

ERIE RAILWAY

And its Connections is unsurpassed by any Route to or from the EAST.

IF ON A BUSINESS TRIP, TAKE THE ERIE,
IF ON A PLEASURE TRIP, TAKE THE ERIE,
UNDER ALL CIRCUMSTANCES, TAKE THE ERIE,

And you will travel over a Railway unequalled in facilities for Comfort and Safety.

JNO. N. ABBOTT,   W. H. HURLBURT,
Gen'l Pass. Agent, NEW YORK.   Gen'l Western Pass. Agent, CHICAGO

THE
Chicago and Atlantic

RAILWAY

IS NOT EXCELLED, IF EQUALLED,

BY ANY OTHER ROAD IN THE WORLD.

SOLID TRAINS

The finest ever built, run between New York and Chicago, and Chicago and New York, daily, via the Erie Railway, without change for any class of passengers. Also, new Pullman Sleeping Cars between

CHICAGO AND BOSTON, VIA ALBANY.

This is the only line running a "solid" train between the above cities. By the term "solid" we mean the entire train—baggage car, first and second-class coaches, smoking car and sleeping cars. The trains are of uniform external appearance; the interior is the perfection of railroad appointment. Even

THE SMOKING CARS

Among other novelties, contain a BUFFET, where the traveler may

LUNCH AT HIS LEISURE.

The trains are fitted with every appliance for

SAFETY and COMFORT

That the requirements of modern travel have prompted inventive genius to provide.

The Sleeping, Drawing-Room and Thoroughfare Coaches are simply Models of Elegance, and are Lighted with the brilliant

PINTSCH GASLIGHT.

In short, the construction, equipment and service of

THE CHICAGO & ATLANTIC

with the advantages it enjoys in connections and time between the

EAST AND WEST,

Necessarily make it the favorite THROUGH LINE to and from the Atlantic Seaboard.

B. F. POPPLE,　　　　　　　　　　**S. W. SNOW,**
Gen'l Eastern Passenger Agent,　　　Gen'l Passenger Agent,
336 BROADWAY, NEW YORK.　　　　　　　CHICAGO.

"One-Third of Life is Spent in Bed."

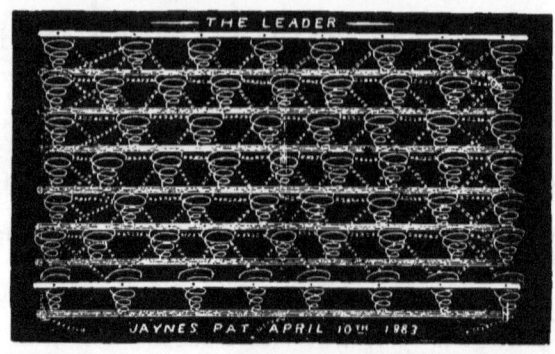

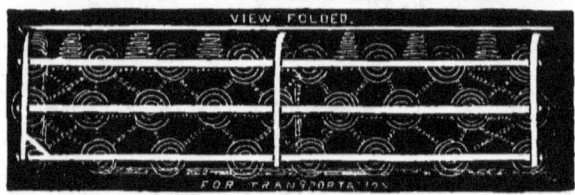

TO SECURE COMFORT, BUY THE

Leader × Metallic × Bed × Spring

PATENTED APRIL 10, 1883.

IT IS THE BEST, because:

First.—Being made entirely of Iron and Steel, it is INSECT PROOF.

Second.—The upper wire of the spiral is DOUBLE-LOOPED; cannot spread under pressure; retains its shape, strength and elasticity.

Third.—The spirals are firmly riveted at the bottom, and at the top are held in position by chains.

Fourth.—The two parts of the cross-bands are connected by pieces of spring steel, so that the Bed Spring can be FOLDED DOUBLE.

Fifth.—A child ten years of age can handle it.

Sixth.—It is INDESTRUCTIBLE.

On application, by mail or otherwise, we will send and take measure of Bedstead. Sold on approval, subject to easy payments, or discount for cash. **SATISFACTION GUARANTEED.**

WELLS & BRO.,

197 Desplaines Street, Chicago.

AT RETAIL

PAPER

HANGINGS

OF

Every Variety.

John J. McGrath,

106, 108, 110, 112 Wabash Ave.

CHICAGO.

www.ingramcontent.com/pod-product-compliance
Lightning Source LLC
Chambersburg PA
CBHW030356170426
43202CB00010B/1392